Misplaced Anger

Lois Kerr

BookLocker
Trenton, Georgia

Print ISBN: 978-1-958891-11-7
Ebook ISBN: 979-8-88531-600-2

Published by BookLocker.com, Inc., Trenton, Georgia.

The characters and events in this book are fictitious. Any similarity to real persons, living or dead, is coincidental and not intended by the author.

BookLocker.com, Inc.
2023

First Edition

Library of Congress Cataloguing in Publication Data
Kerr, Lois
Misplaced Anger by Lois Kerr
Library of Congress Control Number: 2023918961

Dedication

To my wonderful husband, Steve.
His support is what helped me do this.

Chapter One

Kester, Illinois, population 88,714, give or take a few. It was a typical mid-sized city anywhere in the United States. From factories to supermarkets, newspapers, good-sized medical centers, pharmacies, hair salons and barbershops, three high schools with eight feeder schools, one university, sit-down restaurants, fast food restaurants, and churches of all denominations, Kester had everything you need in a city to grow and thrive.

The population of Kester here in the year 2000 was very diverse. You had white collar to blue collar to no collar. The unemployment rate was low as was the crime rate. Churches were full on Sunday mornings.

A few well-to-do families owned the primary industries and entertainment in Kester.

The city's most prominent corporation was Martin Metal Fabrication. It employed about half the people in the city in one capacity or another, from office workers to assembly line employees to transport drivers. The factory produced panels for the back of most major appliances. It also created the screws, washers, and nuts to attach the panels. The products were shipped worldwide. Consequently, the wages and benefits were pretty good for the factory.

The same family had owned the factory for over one hundred years. The owners were Patrick and Peg Martin. They had one son, James. At eighteen he would be entering his second year of college. He was studying business so he could take over the factory when his father retired.

This city was large enough to support a good daily newspaper. *The News-Sentinel.* The owners of the newspaper were the Bakers. They had two children, Trinity, eighteen, and Brandon, twenty six.

There were six Saver's Supermarkets. The Sanders owned them all. They had one son, Derek, eighteen.

The Perkins were the fast food franchise "King & Queen." They owned four Burger King restaurants and a couple of high-end Italian restaurants, Marianna's and Italian East. They had one daughter, Missy, eighteen.

The Cassidys owned much of the entertainment in town, including Scene It, a 10-Plex Movie Theater, and next door, Galaxy Strikes and Spares, a sixteen-lane bowling alley. They had one son, Andrew, nineteen.

The Romans owned a string of Speedway gas stations. It's said they made more money from their lottery sales than from gas. Their son, Matt, was eighteen.

The six privileged teenagers had been friends since grade school. All were looking forward to summer now that school was out. James and Trinity had been a couple on and off through high school and now college.

David Parker was forty-seven. His wife, Sharon, was forty-two. They'd been married for almost twenty years. They had three children, Laura, eighteen, studying business administration in her first year of college, and eleven-year-old twins, Elizabeth and Jeremiah.

David had worked at Martin Metal Fabrication for ten years. He brought home a decent paycheck working the assembly line on the 7-3:30 shift. He wasn't a big man, only five-foot-nine, but strong for his size. With his dark hair and blue eyes he could have been any other man in a crowd, but to Sharon and the children he was their world.

Sharon had worked for the Martins as a domestic for about six years. She was a small woman, only five-foot-three. She had sandy blond hair and gray eyes that just glowed when she smiled.

Laura was petite like her mother, only a little over five feet tall and weighed just a little over one hundred pounds. Like many other teenagers she wore her brown hair long. Her blue eyes stood out to anyone who met her.

Elizabeth was small and athletic. Her hair was very blond compared to even her mother's, but her eyes were like her mother's, gray and sparkly. Jeremiah was inching toward being tall like his father. His hair was also blond but closer to the shade of his mother's. Unlike everyone else in the family, his eyes were more hazel. They both had an impish grin.

Sunday mornings were family time. The Parkers were devout Catholics. Morning mass came before anything. Sharon especially believed in the power of prayer. There wasn't much that couldn't be accomplished if you prayed hard enough.

On Wednesday nights David went with his friends to the Moose Lodge where they were all members to play euchre and unwind. David wasn't much of a drinker but did have an occasional beer with the guys.

Also on Wednesday Sharon met with a large group of ladies to knit or crochet blankets for babies coming home from the hospital. They also sewed quilts for residents of the local nursing home. Once a year they made "Quilts of Valor" for local veterans.

Together on Sunday night, they bowled in a mixed doubles league.

Weather permitting they rode their bikes along the city's bike trails with their children.

Chapter 2

Spring is pretty fickle in Central Illinois. It'll be eighty degrees one day and then temperatures drop and the next day is cold and snowy. When the weather is nice people really take advantage of it. Bikes come from the garage and people wear shorts and T-shirts. House windows are opened to let in some fresh air.

This Tuesday in late April was one of those lovely warm days.

It would be warm for his ride home at 3:30 p.m. David Parker was happy he could ride his bike to work, and after working his shift. The Parkers only had one car. On Tuesday Sharon would take David to work early so she could get to her job at 6:30 a.m. This Tuesday though Sharon was tickled that she could just drive to work on time. Sharon was glad she didn't have to hurry through her second job to get David from work.

Sharon was one of the four domestics at Martin Manor along with Charles Testor, the chauffeur, and Benjamin Rose, Miss Peg's personal assistant.

Besides being a domestic at Martin Manor she also cleaned three other houses during the week. The money from these three houses was different from regular living money.

It sounded like Sharon was doing all the work but that isn't the case. Usually, you could see David doing dishes and cleaning the kitchen after supper so Sharon could sit down for a while.

The love between David and Sharon was undeniable. A quick hug or kiss as they passed each other was a regular thing, much to the disgust of the twins. Sometimes it was just a look from across a room that let you know their souls were intertwined. They never parted ways without a kiss and an "I love you" on their lips. They felt the last words that they should hear from each other was "I love you" if something should happen, heaven forbid.

David and Sharon were determined their three children would do better than they were doing. Much of their income was going to special accounts specifically for their college educations.

Laura had proven to them so far that their money was being well spent. She has pulled straight As and made the dean's list in her first year of college.

The twins were headed into middle school with grades just as impressive. Elizabeth had straight As. Jeremiah got one B and the rest As.

There was going to be a big cookout that weekend to celebrate everyone's grades and the end of the school year.

Laura was happily cooking dinner this Tuesday. She was ending her first year of college and she wanted to thank her parents for making that happen. It wouldn't be anything fancy but any time Sharon didn't have to cook it was appreciated.

At about 3 p.m. Mike Forrest dropped off his laundry. This was job number three for Sharon, and was one that Laura helped with. There were a lot of single people in Kester who lived in apartments. Doing their own laundry was something they weren't great at doing. They dropped the laundry off to Sharon and picked it up two days later all washed and folded. The washer and dryer at the Parkers' home ran about six days a week. Sharon just hoped the machines would last a while.

Laura had just started frying the onions and ground beef for the goulash she was making when Sharon got home. It was 3:30 p.m.

Sharon: "Mmm, that smells good. I love the smell of onions cooking."

Laura: "Take your shoes off and put your feet up while I take care of this. Elizabeth and Jeremiah are out back with a couple of friends….And, yes, they changed their school clothes. They said they're glad to be out of them for the summer."

Sharon did take off her shoes but grabbed Mike's laundry to get it started. There was no slowing her down.

Sharon: "Dad should be home a little after four. It does take him a little longer to get home when he rides his bike."

Laura: "He may be on his feet all day but his legs will be sore tonight. He isn't used to peddling his bike that far. He'll really enjoy his iced tea tonight."

Everyone went about what they were doing and lost track of time. The twins came in and asked where Dad was. They figured he would be home by now...it was 4:15 p.m. He was late. Sharon figured it was just taking longer than usual because he stopped somewhere or the traffic was heavy.

4:30 p.m. Still waiting for Dad. Sharon was starting to worry.

5:00 p.m. A knock at the front door. Standing there were two Kester police officers.

The twins came running thinking it was Dad....then stopped in their tracks. Laura came up behind them.

First officer: "Mrs. Parker, there's been an accident. You need to come with us to the hospital."

Sharon's face turned white. A groan escaped her lips as she staggered back against the wall beside the door. She stared at the officers and then at the children with a pained look on her face.

Sharon: (With a tremble in her voice) "First, tell me what this is about. My husband... is he all right?"

Second officer: "You should really just come with us. We can explain on the way."

Sharon: "NO, I need to know. Is he okay?"

Neither of the officers felt they could answer her at this point. The looks on their faces though just about said it all. David was not okay.

Laura: "Mom, let's just all go to the hospital. I can drive us. I don't think the twins should be left here and I'm certainly not staying here. Kids, get into the car. Officers, could you get us there quickly through traffic?"

First officer: "Sure. It's probably better if you drive."

The ride to the hospital was unreal. There was a police car in front and one in back of the little Ford Falcon—a classic '60s car—as it sped through town toward the hospital. A drive that would typically take twenty minutes took half that. Laura's eyes were focused ahead at the taillights of the police car. Hard telling how many red lights they flew through or how fast they had been driving.

Everyone froze in their seats as they pulled up to the ER at St. Ignatius Medical Center. They knew they needed to go inside but no one wanted to go.

The officer in the first police car came up to the driver's door and opened it.

First officer: "Gather your family and go in. I'll park your car."

Laura just looked up at him. Her firm resolve was starting to crumble. She looked up at the officer but couldn't say anything. He took her hand and smiled ever so slightly, then helped her stand and steady herself. That was the help she needed at that moment. She smiled back at him and joined her family to walk into the hospital.

Chapter 3

St. Ignatius Medical Center was a good size for a city of this population. Their trauma center in the ER was one of the best in the state.

Walking into the large ER was very intimidating. Stark-white walls and shiny tile floors showed they cared about appearance. There was no mistaking the smell of alcohol and disinfectant.

Two different police officers were standing just inside the large sliding doors.

First officer: "Mrs. Parker?"

Sharon: "Yes, where is my husband? The other officers said he's been in an accident. I want to see him. How bad was he hurt?"

First officer: "Let me take you back where we can talk privately and I'll explain everything."

Sharon: "Okay, but you aren't answering my question...how badly was he hurt?"

The officer gently takes her arm, directs her and the children to a quiet lounge area, and closes the door.

First officer: "Mrs. Parker, I'm afraid I have some bad news. Your husband was hit on Broadway by a hit-and-run driver. Witnesses said the impact threw him to the sidewalk that runs along the road. Apparently, he landed head-first on the concrete. Someone called 911 while a couple of people attempted CPR. They kept it up until the EMTs could take over but they could not revive him. I'm sorry but he died at the scene. Between the concussion and his broken neck, I'm sure he died quickly."

Sharon: "NOOO! That can't be. You've made a horrible mistake. I want to see him…NOW."

It seemed like Sharon's legs became jelly as she collapsed to the floor. The officer caught her before she hit the floor. The children rushed to her side all crying at once. The officer got her safely into a chair.

Once Sharon regained her composure they were all led back to the room where David had been taken. His face had at least been washed so the family didn't see most of the blood. He was severely bruised and swollen.

Sharon lay over him quietly sobbing while Laura just stood there and stared while holding the twins in her arms. Elizabeth was crying softly. Jeremiah though was sobbing so hard he seemed unable to stop. He and his father were very close. There was no comforting him.

The rest of the evening was a blur. For as compassionate as they were, the nurses still had tough questions. They gave Sharon a bag with his personal items, wallet, keys, and lunch box. This just brought on more sobbing. Then they asked which funeral home she wanted David to be sent to.

Sharon: "McCullough's I guess. It's the nicest I can think of."

It took all she could do for Laura to pull Sharon and the twins out of the hospital. It's hard to leave the most important person in your world broken and alone.

The police officer brought the car around for the family. They had all been so kind and thoughtful through all of this. To say "Thank you" never seems to be enough. He saw this family at the worst time of their lives. Their compassion toward them could never be repaid.

Laura: "Do you know who did this to my dad? Is there any information on the car or the driver? Did anyone see anything?"

First officer: "Right now we don't know anything. We've been interviewing witnesses but it happened so quickly that no one remembers anything. I'm sorry I don't have more for you. I know that doesn't help. We'll let you know if we get any information that might help."

Laura: "Thank you. I know you will. Again, thank you for all you've done."

Chapter 4

Laura drove home in a daze. Sharon just stared out the window. Elizabeth sighed and cried softly. Jeremiah was still sobbing, cuddled next to his sister.

What started out as a beautiful, happy sunny day had turned into a nightmare and it was still only 8 p.m.

Laura knew that she would have to pull herself together and become the strong one to get the family through all of this.

She got the twins to get ready for bed. Amazingly they didn't put up a fight. Once that was done she made Sharon a cup of bedtime tea. The ER doctor gave her a couple of pills to help Sharon sleep so she could move through this haze that now surrounded them.

Once they were all ready for bed the twins wanted to sleep with Sharon. They didn't want to be alone.

Laura: "Okay, pile in. Mom, is that all right with you?"

Sharon: "Yes, let me hold my babies tonight."

Laura: "Now that you're all settled I need to run an errand. I won't be long."

Sharon: "Where could you possibly need to go right now that can't wait until tomorrow?"

Laura: "Don't worry, Mom. It's important. I'll explain it in the morning. You all settle in and try to get some sleep. I love you all. Good night."

With hugs and kisses for all, Laura closed the bedroom door, grabbed her purse and keys, and headed out the door.

Chapter 5

Martin Manor was a very imposing structure just on the outskirts of town. It sat on a sprawling estate of around ten acres. The mansion sat in an area where most of the Kester elite resided. It was the largest and oldest private residence in Kester. Considering the fact that the Martins were the wealthiest in town made all of this apparent. The Martins were old money though. All the others were new money. Built in the early 1800s the craftsmanship was impressive. Every stone on the outside was obtained from the surrounding countryside and river bottom. The men who had built this mansion were taught their crafts in Europe and took pride in their work.

A large porch surrounded the front and one side of the structure. Two large, heavy doors opened to a wide, open foyer. To the right of the foyer was a massive library. Bookshelves extended from the floor up to the ten-foot ceilings. The shelves contained many first-edition volumes that had probably never been opened. On the left of the foyer was a magnificent sitting room. With a fireplace on one wall the room felt very warm. All the overstuffed furniture made just sitting in this room very comfortable. On the left side of the massive staircase was a commercial-size kitchen. The size made it possible for the staff to prepare meals for a large number of guests or just the family and staff.

The area under the massive staircase held two rooms. One room was Miss Peg's study. The other room held Benjamin's small office. Miss Peg liked being close to everything going on in the house, so this area was perfect for her.

To the right of the staircase past the library was the ballroom. For many years in the past there were balls and parties held in this room. A lot of joy moved through this house. Upstairs there were eight bedrooms and just as many baths. Each bedroom had a large four-poster bed and heavy drapes to hold out the light. Claw foot tubs were in some bathrooms while a couple were updated to showers. The wallpaper throughout the mansion looked very Victorian. One of the daily jobs of the staff was to dust down all the walls to keep them fresh and clean.

It was about a fifteen-minute drive to the Martins' home. Laura felt she needed to let Miss Peg know what was going on. Miss Peg (everyone called her that by her request; she said Mrs. Martin was her mother-in-law) would want to know what had happened immediately. For one thing, she needed to know that Sharon would be off for an extended period of time. Most importantly she needed to know the reason why.

The other reason was she needed to talk to Benjamin, Miss Peg's personal assistant.

Miss Peg was like everyone's mother. She took care of people as if they were her own family. She looked her age of fifty-two. Standing about five-foot-three, she had black hair but was starting to gray at the temples. It was obvious that she enjoyed the many wonderful meals and especially all the sweets prepared by her great cooks. The clothes she wore were very conservative; you might call them frumpy. She had a smile though that made you feel safe and comfortable. One look into her eyes let you know that you mattered to her.

It was about 10 p.m. when Laura steeled herself to knock on the front door. This would be the first time she would say out loud what had happened today. She was getting pretty shaky by the time Miss Peg opened the door.

Miss Peg: "My goodness, child, what brings you out at this time of night?"

Laura: "Miss Peg, I'm sorry to bother you this late but I need to tell you something and...well...kinda need your help."

Miss Peg: "You look like you're about to collapse. Come to the kitchen, I'll make us some tea while you tell me what is happening."

Once they were settled in the kitchen...no one said anything at this point...Laura finally let the floodgates open. What started out as simply crying turned into sobbing. Miss Peg set down the tea and pulled a chair next to Laura. She pulled her into her arms and let her cry herself out. Once Laura was able to stop she told Miss Peg what she came to say to her.

Laura: "This is the first time I've had to say this out loud. I'm not sure how. At about four o'clock today, on his way home from work (sob), my dad was hit on his bike and killed by a hit-and-run driver. (Really crying by now.) According to the police, he was thrown and landed on his head. He sustained a severely crushed skull, a broken neck, and a lot of other injuries. Bystanders tried to help him but it was too late."

"They haven't given us any information about the car or driver. Well, if they had I really wasn't listening. All I knew then was that my dad wasn't coming home."

The shock on Miss Peg's face was undeniable. The gasp she let out showed that.

Miss Peg: "Oh my God. Cry it out, sweet child. This is something you can't keep bundled up. I'm here to help."

She got up from her chair and tightly enveloped Laura in her arms. Laura crumbled and cried like she couldn't stop.

Miss Peg: "How is your mother? She must be beside herself. And how are the twins?"

Laura: "Mom is a mess. She didn't say two words on the way home from the hospital. You know she probably won't be back to work for a while. Elizabeth is not doing well. Jeremiah is inconsolable right now. He was still softly sobbing when I left. One of the ER doctors gave me a mild sedative to help Mom get some sleep. They were all curled in her bed when I left."

"Besides telling you one of the reasons I came was to see if Benjamin could help me sort through our finances since that is what he does. I need to see where I can pull money from our college accounts to pay for Dad's funeral. Then I need help with some sort of budget since we will no longer have Dad's paycheck."

Miss Peg: "You are wise beyond your years to think about all of this when I know your head is probably spinning right now."

Laura: "I don't have a choice. Mom is a basket case so nothing would get done. I guess some of the classes I have taken so far in college stuck. That's the only reason I have for that. I was studying business. I need something to keep my mind busy or I'll collapse."

Miss Peg: "Okay, I will help you out here. Both of your parents work for us in some capacity. We take care of our own. Do not worry about the cost of the funeral. I will handle everything. Your mother is very special to me. I've never seen a harder worker. I wouldn't have it any other way. You shouldn't have to worry about this right now. You take care of your family and let me do this. Where did they take him?"

Laura: "McCullough's. That was the only decision I think my mom was capable of making at the time. I didn't come here to ask you for this though. I really can't expect you to do this. You have no obligation to us."

Miss Peg: "You didn't ask and I know that wasn't why you came here. We all need help and a shoulder to lean on now and then. I'm very glad you came and let me know. I want to help find and punish the person who did this horrible thing to your family."

"I will call and get all the arrangements taken care of. The only thing you and your mother will have to do is unfortunately write the obituary and decide what clothes you want him to wear. I haven't said it yet, Laura, but I am so sorry. I hope they find the coward that did this and make them pay for what they have done."

Little did anyone know at the time that it would never happen as one would expect.

Laura: "Thank you. I will still need Benjamin's help to work out our budget. Losing a paycheck will hurt. I've already decided I won't go back to school this year. It won't be in the budget. By some slim chance would you have a position open that I can fill? I'm going to need a job to help out. Don't answer now. I don't want to put you on the spot. You might have another suggestion anyway."

"Right now I need to get back home Hopefully everyone is asleep. I started cooking supper before this happened so I need to clean the kitchen. I don't want Mom waking up to that. Thank you, Miss Peg. We don't have any family here so you were the person I thought might be able to help screw my head back on straight...and you did. You've lifted a lot off my shoulders. I do need to go make a couple of phone calls yet tonight. I need to notify a few people before it gets much later. There is no way I'll ever be able to repay you."

Miss Peg: "You don't worry about that now. You have enough on your plate. Go get some rest. Leave everything else to me."

With a lot of hugging Miss Peg finally walked Laura to her car. Miss Peg's heart was breaking for this young family. Laura's strength surprised her. She would make sure somehow that they didn't have to struggle too much in the coming weeks.

Chapter 6

When Laura got home she checked on her mom and the twins. They were all wrapped together in a ball in the middle of the bed. That was the only bright spot in the day.

She sat down to make the phone calls she had been dreading. The first was to her Uncle Daniel, her dad's brother. The scream on the other end of the line was expected. He had all the questions she didn't have the answers to yet. She told him she would call him back when everything was finalized. She also called Mom's sister, Aunt Connie. Same questions from her. She said she would be here tomorrow to help Sharon get through this.

The following week was pretty much a blur. Miss Peg was true to her word. The funeral planning was flawless. All Sharon and Laura had to do was get David's suit to the funeral home.

DAVID PARKER, 47,

died Tuesday, April 14, 2000, as a result of a vehicle accident.

David was born Aug. 4, 1953, in Kester to John and Mary Parker who have preceded him in death.

He married Sharon Klinger on July 16, 1980. She survives along with his children, Laura, Elizabeth, and Jeremiah. Also surviving is one brother, Daniel.

David was an active member of the Moose Lodge #133 where he met with friends for a weekly game of euchre.

David worked at Martin Metal Fabrication for over ten years where he developed many friendships over those years.

Many weekends you could find him at someone's house helping with anything from fixing a roof to building a storage shed.

David deeply loved his wife and children. He could be

seen on family biking treks or sledding down a snowy hill.

He was a lifelong member of St. Michael's Catholic Church.

Family and friends may call from 3 p.m. to 7 p.m. Friday, April 17, 2000, at McCullough Memorial Chapel, 1842 Spring St. where a rosary will be recited at 4:30 p.m. Visitation will also take place at St. Michael's Catholic Church from 10 a.m. until Mass on Saturday.

A Mass of Christian Burial will be celebrated at 11 a.m. Saturday. Burial will follow at Grace Serenity Gardens.

It was amazing how many people knew David. There was a line at the funeral home for the viewing. There were so many flowers that they were not just around the casket but around the entire room. David was obviously loved by a lot more people than even Sharon realized. It raised her heart to know this.

St. Michael's Catholic Church was packed for the funeral mass. The procession to Grace Serenity Gardens held up most intersections for twenty minutes. David was going to his final resting place in style.

A couple of days after the funeral Sheriff Mark Stone stopped by the house to update Sharon on the accident. As of this point, there were no new leads as to who the driver could be. All the witnesses told them was that they thought it was a silver car. The police had contacted all the body shops in town to be on the lookout for a silver car with right front-end damage. None of the witnesses to the accident remembered what kind of car it was. Some people thought it might have been a luxury car but it all happened so fast that no one could be sure. Sheriff Stone was saying it could be someone driving through town.

In the back of his mind though he had another thought. It just wasn't something he could say out loud right now.

Miss Peg spoke to Benjamin about Laura's request. He took on the request without question.

Sharon returned to work at the Martins three weeks after the accident. Laura went with her and Miss Peg put her under Joanne's wing in the kitchen. Joanne ran the kitchen for the Martin family so was always happy for the help. Along with Nancy, the other kitchen aide, the kitchen was now well-staffed.

The other domestics—Cynthia, Mary, and Bethany—rallied around Sharon to make returning to work easier. These ladies were all very close so they also wanted to support Sharon and Laura as much as possible. Things would never be the same but the ladies wanted to get things back to normal as soon as possible, whatever that normal might be.

A few days after Sharon returned to work Benjamin said he needed to talk to her about their new budget.

At the end of the day, Sharon and Laura stayed to talk to Benjamin. He was all smiles when they walked into his office.

Benjamin at forty-two had been Miss Peg's assistant for the last ten years. She trusted him implicitly. Looking at him you would think of Radar from the TV series *M*A*S*H*. He was a small man with thinning strawberry blond hair wearing wire-rimmed glasses that he seemed to be adjusting all the time.

Benjamin: "Come in, sit down. I have some good news for you. I know there isn't much to be happy about right now but I think my news will help."

Sharon: "First of all I want to thank you for helping us out. Our minds really aren't too down to earth right now."

Benjamin: "It's my pleasure. It felt good to have something to dig into. Working for Miss Peg doesn't keep me all that busy. You can only finance so many tea parties. Anyway, your husband really was a forward-thinker. All employees of Martin Metal automatically have $3,000 of life insurance. The company figured it would help the family a little when someone dies. The employees also have the option for more insurance if they want to pay an extra premium. David paid the extra premium. He was paying on a $200,000 life insurance policy. The insurance company will have no problem paying it since he's had the policy for so many years. I'm sure this will help you back on your feet. We can work on your budget after this."

David wanted to make sure his family was cared for if something ever happened. His own father had died when he was a teenager. He left them with nothing but bills since he spent the bill money at the bars. He, his mother, and his brother struggled to make ends meet for years. David didn't want this for his family.

Sharon couldn't speak. Even in death, David took care of her and the children. Laura took over.

Laura: "What do we need to do next? We can give you the authority to get into any of our accounts to get this all done if that's what you need."

Benjamin: "That will be fine. I'll get all this started in the morning. Maybe you can sleep a little easier tonight knowing David is still caring for you and at least some of your finances will be in order."

Sharon: "First thing I want you to do is to take the money to pay Miss Peg back for David's funeral."

Benjamin: "That won't happen. Miss Peg felt it was an honor to be able to do this for your family. She loves to do what she can for her staff. She's paid off mortgages to avoid foreclosures and paid for surgeries in the past for employees. No one knows what she does or for whom, but she feels she needs to do it. So, even trying to pay her back won't work. I think she would feel insulted if you did."

Sharon and Laura left in disbelief. First that David was still taking care of them even beyond the grave. Second, Miss Peg thought so much of them that she was taking care of them, too.

As they were leaving they ran into James.

James: "Hey, Dogpatch, how are you doing?"

James was pretty oblivious to anyone around who wasn't in his group of friends. He started calling Laura that when he realized that he'd seen her on the campus last year and now she worked for his mother. In his mind, anyone not in his circle wasn't worth his time. To him, they were not much more than hillbillies. He had no idea what Laura had been through and didn't care. He would tease and humiliate her any chance he got. He really wasn't a nice person. This would go on for years.

James at eighteen was a nice enough looking young man. His arrogance and nasty attitude though took away from his looks. At six-foot-two he carried his one 190 pounds very well. His hair was black like his mother's and very thick. His brown eyes only reflected his contempt of most people around him.

Chapter 7

Within a week Benjamin had everything straightened out. The Parkers had been in their house for twenty years so they had to have the mortgage well paid down. Benjamin helped Sharon pay off the mortgage completely. He then worked out the schedule for them to save for the taxes and insurance.

Sharon was able to buy a new washer and dryer. She did so much laundry she wasn't sure how long the old ones would last.

Next Laura talked her into buying a new car. David's 1968 Falcon was starting to nickel and dime them to death. They really needed a more reliable one.

That was all the major purchases they needed to make. The rest of the money, actually a nice chunk, went to college accounts. They didn't have to scrimp and save at least now with Benjamin's new budget.

Charles went with Sharon to get a car since she knew little to nothing about cars. Coincidentally there was a man there interested in buying the Falcon. It was a classic and he wanted to restore it. He gave Sharon a good price for it. That prompted her to buy a better car than she originally planned.

For the time being they didn't need to concern themselves about the ability to afford to live day to day. David made sure of that.

Chapter 8

Everyday life for the Parker family took a while to come to pass. The school was out for the summer so keeping busy became a challenge. A lot of sleepovers kept the twins busy for at least a couple of days a week. Their friends sensed they needed a good distraction.

Sharon started meeting again with her quilting and stitching friends. Sewing was one of her passions so at least that was one thing that made her happy.

Laura also picked up a couple of houses to clean. She was determined to pull her weight. Every dollar helped. That would be truer than she could have imagined.

Again Miss Peg took care of the Parkers. She gave her entire staff a raise so giving Sharon and Laura a large one didn't raise any questions. Sharon felt they were back on track with the twins' college funds. She didn't want them in debt when they got out of school.

Once school started back the twins were pretty busy. As usual, their grades were at the top of their classes so they, too, were back on track.

As the years ticked by, the grief of losing David started to calm down. At first, Jeremiah would wake up screaming. He never had nightmares before David died. After about a year and talking to the parish priest the nightmares eventually stopped. That was the year they also heard about early college classes. They could take them right along with their high school classes. The significant part about the program was that the class costs were included in their high school tuition. So, instead of paying $75-150 a credit hour in college, the cost was barely felt.

At this point, the twins had turned fourteen and were pretty sure what their career path would be.

Jeremiah was determined to become a master chef, studying around the world. He decided he would own a high-end restaurant. You know, the kind where you need reservations and still may have to stand in line.

Elizabeth was determined to work herself up to a PA (Physician's Assistant). With her grades, there was no doubt she would get there.

With some classes under their belt, they were both on their way to their dream.

Chapter 9

This particular winter the twins had plenty of time to study since they were home-bound with a cold and the flu. Laura caught a minor cold. It wasn't bad enough though to keep her from working or caring for the family.

Sharon was a different story though. The flu got hold of her and really held on. She had been off for about six days. Laura came home from work and checked on her. Sharon was struggling to breathe. Without hesitation, Laura called an ambulance. She then called the neighbor Miss Beatrice to intercept the twins and let them know what was going on.

Within ten minutes Sharon was on her way to St. Ignatius Medical Center. Laura was right behind. This trip was too much like this same trip three years ago but Laura was trying to keep those thoughts out of her mind. She just kept saying, "This is different—Mom is alive and will be just fine. She just needs a little help to get through this."

Miss Beatrice brought the twins to the hospital and then left. She said to call her if they needed anything else.

It seemed like forever before they were allowed to go to the room to see her. She had an IV going and was hooked up to a monitor. According to the monitor, the oxygen mask wasn't giving her enough.

Doctor: "We're going to have to put her on a vent then send her up to ICU. She'll be here for a while. Once she's on the vent she won't be able to talk but will be awake. We won't sedate her unless we need to."

It was another couple of hours before they were able to see her. The twins were too young to go into ICU but Laura explained to the nurses about their dad so they relented.

Nurse: "Just keep quiet while you're in her room. I'm not about to keep kids from seeing their mom."

There were rules about how long they could be on the unit. After about a half hour the nurse came in and told them that they did have to leave. They all kissed her and left. The nurse told Laura she would call if there were any changes. Reluctantly they left and went home.

The drive home was a silent one. No one thought they could sleep but they went to bed with heavy hearts.

The phone rang at about 2 a.m.

Nurse: "Miss Parker, your mother is not doing well. I think you should come in."

Laura: "Thank you. We'll be there as soon as we can."

Laura went in and woke up the twins.

Laura: "Get up. I just got a call from the hospital. Mom isn't doing well. We need to get to the hospital. Get dressed quick."

They were ready and out of the house in less than five minutes. Laura drove carefully but fast...well over the speed limit to get to the hospital as quickly as she could.

The unit was quiet at this time of night except for the sounds of the monitors beeping. The nurse saw them get off the elevator and met them.

Nurse: "I'm sorry to have to call you in the middle of the night, but felt you should be here. Your Mom's condition has greatly deteriorated."

She pulled Laura aside.

Nurse: "She isn't doing well, at all. I hate to put it this way but I think you should all go in and say your goodbyes. I don't think she has much more time. All her vitals keep dropping. Even on the vent she is struggling. You can all go in now. Talk to her and be positive. I can't tell you if she can hear you but if she can you would want her to hear happy thoughts from her children."

Laura and the twins went into Sharon's room. The only sounds were the monitors and the vent that was breathing for her.

Elizabeth was on one side of her and Jeremiah was on the other side while Laura stood at the foot of the bed. They all just stood there for a minute talking gently to let Sharon know they were there.

Laura suggested they all say some prayers. Sharon was a big believer in praying so hopefully this would comfort her.

They started with the Lord's Prayer.

Laura, Elizabeth, and Jeremiah: "Our Father, who art in heaven, hallowed be thy name; thy kingdom come; thy will be done; on earth as it is in heaven. Give us this day our daily bread. And forgive us our trespasses, as we forgive those who trespass against us. And lead us not into temptation, but deliver us from evil. Amen."

At this point, the nurse had called in the hospital chaplain to give Sharon last rites.

The children continued to pray. Sharon's grip on the children's hands seemed to get stronger after this. Keep going.

Laura, Elizabeth, and Jeremiah: "Hail Mary, Full of Grace, The Lord is with thee. Blessed art thou among women, and blessed is the fruit of thy womb, Jesus. Holy Mary, Mother of God, pray for us sinners now, and at the hour of death."

A tear rolled down Sharon's cheek as they finished. It seemed to be what she had been waiting for. As soon as they said Amen, Sharon took her last breath.

They were able to say their "I love yous" to her but she never regained consciousness. They knew she heard them though and said goodbye in her own way.

The children stood next to her bed in pain and shock. They finally went and sat down in the waiting room where they could let out their emotions. It didn't seem like any of them could stop crying. Laura sat with one of them on each side of her. They sat there until they could calm down. Without saying anything she got them up and out to the car. It seemed like a very long ride home.

Everyone got tucked into bed to try and sleep. The next several days would not be pleasant.

It was 3:30 a.m. but Laura needed to call her Aunt Connie and Uncle Daniel right away. Everyone else could wait until morning. Aunt Connie was obviously upset and had questions. She said she'd be there the next day to take care of them. Laura would answer the questions then. All Laura could say was "thank you" for coming so quickly. She needed the support.

She sat there for a couple of minutes until she had the strength to get up and go to bed. She was not looking forward to the days to come.

Again she would go see Miss Peg and let her know about Sharon and get some much-needed advice.

This one wasn't any easier than the one she made when her dad died. This time though was early morning and all the staff were present. The gasps and tears came quickly. She had the twins with her so they were enveloped in the arms of all the people who knew Sharon the most. As the saying goes: There wasn't a dry eye in the house.

Chapter 10

No one was aware of how sick Sharon really was. Sharon may have been the only one who knew. She hadn't been herself since David was killed. She didn't smile or laugh as freely. The last three years she seemed to sink more and more into herself. Even though she was a small woman, she was pretty strong. Lately though, she seemed increasingly frail. Her rock and soulmate, David was gone and she was just floating through life.

Laura: "Kids, I need to go talk to Miss Peg and Benjamin. Ladies, can they stay with you for a little while?"

In unison as if scripted they all said "Yes" and proceeded to get something for the children to eat. Joanne, the head of the kitchen went out to tell Charles what had happened. They were both back in less than five minutes keeping Elizabeth and Jeremiah occupied.

Miss Peg was greatly saddened by the news. She pulled Laura into her arms and just let her cry.

Lois Kerr

They then walked back to Benjamin's office. He also was visibly upset to hear the news about Sharon.

Laura: "Benjamin, I need your expertise again to rework our budget. Again we're down a paycheck but I can't let the twins' education suffer because of it. That was one thing my parents were passionate about."

"I know when Dad died Mom went to McCullough's and preplanned her funeral. I also found out, Miss Peg, that they told you about it and you paid for everything. We will forever be in your debt for all you have done for us. I don't know how I will ever repay you."

Miss Peg: "I told you when your father died we take care of our own. I wasn't just whistling through my teeth. I meant it. You're on your own now; you shouldn't have to worry about all of this. You take care of the children, I'll take care of the rest."

Laura: "Thank you, you are too much. (She allowed a small grin to cross her lips.) One other thing, Miss Peg, I'm pretty sure we'll need a lawyer. I'm twenty-one and an adult but the twins are only fourteen. I need to talk to a lawyer to make sure I'm their guardian without any questions. The thought of them going into foster care and being taken away from me is the one thing we all couldn't handle right now. I certainly don't want CPS showing up one day, demanding the kids go with them. Do you know someone you could suggest?"

Miss Peg: "I'll call our attorney, Sam Lancaster. He met with your mother not too long after your dad died. I believe he helped her make up a will. It was understood when your father died that Sharon would control everything since you were all underage. Your mother wanted to make sure the very concerns that you are having right now would be covered. I'll call him in the morning so he can file all the necessary paperwork. By Tuesday all will be signed and legal. This is the one thing you can keep out of your mind. He's very intelligent so will know exactly what needs to be done to ease your mind."

Just then James and Trinity Baker walked in.

James: "Well if it isn't Dogpatch, here on a Saturday. I see you have the two Mud Puddles with you, too. What's up?"

Without saying a word, Laura got up from her chair and did something that surprised her and everyone else. She walked up to James and slapped him hard across the face. The slap was hard enough that he stumbled back. James took a step as if he was going to slap her back. That was before Benjamin and Miss Peg quickly stood up. He promptly changed his mind.

James: "Hey! What the hell? Mighty gutsy doing that in front of your boss."

Laura: "I won't put up with your nasty mouth or disrespect today. Your names for all of us are disgusting. I just lost my mother. Those are her children and certainly don't deserve the way you have just referred to them. Say something like that again and I'll match the other side of your face. Keep grinning, Trinity, and you'll be next. I'm sure I could have you on the ground with one slap. Be careful, both of you, grief makes people do the unexpected. I'm not above doing anything unexpected today."

Miss Peg: "Oh my, that is out of character for Laura. James, I think you need to apologize and then leave. This is not the time or the place for your rude behavior."

James: (With his hand on his left cheek) "I'm...I'm sorry. (Even though you could tell it was said sarcastically). Come on, Trinity, let's go before she goes off again. I just came home to pack a bag anyway and get Dad's credit card. We thought we'd take some time off and fly to Vegas. The weather is better out there."

Miss Peg: "You will not get the credit card. You're making a very good salary at the plant. Use your own money to do your gallivanting."

James: (With a strange smile on his face) "Dad will give it to me if I ask nicely. He just wants me to be happy. Anyway, do you really want to discuss this in front of the help? This is a family matter."

With that comment hanging they walked out of the room. But James couldn't resist one last comment.

James: "WOW, just WOW!"

Laura: "Miss Peg, I'm sorry. I don't know what got into me. I don't let my anger get physical. He was just so out of line that I guess my brain took over the wrong way. I'd never say that to Jim though. Even though I surprised even myself by doing that he's had that coming for a long time. Maybe he'll think twice before letting his mouth run off like that."

Miss Peg: "No apology needed. You are right, he had that coming. He's usually too big for his britches. His father has been spoiling him terribly these last few years, for some reason. I've tried to put a stop to it but get overridden. I've also tried to teach him some respect but he is just like Patrick. He can be pretty disrespectful, too, but I've been able to rein him in. James though could have used a couple of trips to the woodshed. One of these days he'll get his comeuppance. It probably won't be pleasant but it will happen."

Laura left right after James and Trinity did. She passed Patrick in the hall on the way out the door. He was on his way to talk to Miss Peg. She had a few choice words for him about the way he was spoiling James.

Patrick: "Was that a friend of James? She looks to be about his age."

Miss Peg: "No, that was Laura, one of my staff. She came to tell me the sad news that her mother passed away last night. She was also a member of my staff."

Patrick: "Trinity said someone slapped James and threatened to slap her as well. Was that the woman?"

Miss Peg: "Yes, his rude and disrespectful comments and behavior was just more than she could deal with today. James has attempted to humiliate her since she started here three years ago. Today he just went too far."

Patrick: "Who is she? Should I know her?"

Miss Peg: "Her name is Laura Parker. She started working for me right after her father was killed by a hit-and-run driver on Broadway. Her mother had already been with me for about three years. Laura left college to come to work to help support their family. James could take lessons from her. Instead he has become more and more abusive."

"Patrick, are you okay? You look very pale. Is it something I said?"

It was true. Patrick sat down and did look very pale. At fifty-eight he more than showed his age. He had been a heavy drinker for many years, causing him to look haggard. At five-foot-nine his weight way overtook his height. All of his suits had started to look just a little tight. His gray hair was almost gone from the top, making him look like a monk but not at all distinguished. There seemed to be a permanent scowl on his face, which just added years to his appearance.

Patrick: "No, I'm fine. I just need some coffee and I'll be on my way. I will say something to James about being more respectful of others."

With that he left. Miss Peg just shook her head and went on with what she needed to do to help with Sharon's funeral.

Chapter 11

Laura and the children left and made their way to what would feel like a very empty house without Sharon. It was a very quiet ride.

SHARON PARKER, 45,
died Friday, October 18, 2003, after a short illness.

Sharon was born February 16, 1958, in Kester to Peter and Melinda Klinger who preceded her in death.

She married David Parker on July 16, 1980. He preceded her in death in 2000. Surviving are her children, Laura, Elizabeth, and Jeremiah. Also surviving is one sister, Constance.

Sharon was an active member of the Kester Sewing Guild which supplied crocheted blankets for newborns and sewn quilts for the elderly.

Sharon worked as a domestic for the Martin family along with keeping up some of the local homes and apartments.

Sharon deeply loved her family and will be sorely missed by all who knew her.

She was a lifelong member of St. Michael's Catholic Church.

Family and friends may call from 3 p.m. to 7 p.m. Sunday, October 20, 2003, at McCullough Memorial Chapel, 1842 Spring St. where a rosary will be recited at 4:30 p.m. Visitation will also take place at St. Michael's Catholic Church from 10 a.m. until Mass on Monday.

A Mass of Christian Burial will be celebrated at 11 a.m. Monday. Burial will follow where she will be laid beside her beloved husband, David, at Grace Serenity Gardens.

As with her dad's funeral, Miss Peg had everything perfect for Sharon's funeral. Miss Peg said all the planning had been done by Sharon but you couldn't miss Miss Peg's influence.

Again it was surprising how many lives Sharon had touched. All the domestics from the wealthier families were at the viewing, mass, and funeral procession. The ladies from her sewing guild were there. The most surprising was all the nurses who stopped to pay their respects. Sharon had gotten to know the nurses from the hospital NICU when she would take the blankets crocheted by the guild. Also many of the nurses from the nursing homes came. The ladies not only made them quilts but spent time with any who may not have had many visitors. Sharon had frequently stopped by just to visit them. The residents themselves would have probably been at the funeral if they could.

Sharon didn't know a stranger. She could make someone's day just with a smile. Her loss would be felt by a lot of people. The Parker children felt a sense of pride, knowing their mother was so special to so many people.

After all these years the police still had no new leads on David's death. It saddened Laura that her mother would never know who took her soulmate. They were together now though as they were always meant to be.

Chapter 12

Just as Laura figured, CPS did show up to check on the children. Apparently, someone from their school had called so they were obligated to visit. All Laura had to do though was show them Sharon's will, her birth certificate proving she was old enough to be their guardian and the papers from the attorney to back it all up. The social worker showed up during the day so the twins never knew about it. That would have upset them unnecessarily.

The next year for the Parker family was challenging. The twins started high school with a cloud over their heads. They'd had the same friends their entire lives. Now in a new school, a lot of their friends went to different high schools. The friends they relied on to perk them up when they felt bad about their parents weren't around. It showed in their grades. Both Elizabeth's and Jeremiah's grades slipped a little. It took some frank talks and family time to get them back on the right track.

Around the same time, things were getting difficult at the Martins' home. Patrick started drinking more than usual. He had been a heavy drinker for years, but it got worse just the last couple of years. He managed to go to work but it was unknown how much he was accomplishing.

Miss Peg was so concerned about his alcohol consumption that she finally took away his car keys. She didn't want to put anyone at risk with him driving drunk. He never seemed sober. Instead of a cup of coffee, he would have a glass of bourbon before leaving for the office. Charles now drove him to the office and picked him up at the end of the day.

One morning in early November Patrick didn't come down to breakfast at his normal time. When Miss Peg went to check on him she found he had been vomiting and was very pale. Actually, he looked jaundiced—yellow instead of white. She called for James to come to help Patrick get cleaned up while she called an ambulance. She figured this was not something that could be fixed by him just staying in bed.

It was during this incident when Miss Peg asked Laura to manage the daily operations at the house. She felt her time and energy should go to caring for Patrick, either here or at the hospital. Under Benjamin's instructions, Laura found out where Miss Peg's calendar and staff paperwork were kept. Everyone had a schedule for the day-to-day operations but Miss Peg had extra daily chores for everyone to keep her house in tip-top condition.

Benjamin was also instructed to not give James any money out of any of the family accounts. Patrick was spoiling James but Miss Peg was determined to put a stop to it.

It turned out that Patrick had developed cirrhosis of the liver from his heavy drinking. The jaundice was only the first sign. After a couple of days in the hospital, his other organs began to shut down.

Within the week Patrick was dead. The mood at the Martin's home was somber, to say the least. Miss Peg didn't speak much if at all. All the staff expressed their heartfelt sympathies to Miss Peg. The staff knew her well enough to know what she needed and when. When she didn't come to a meal they made sure to take it to her. They would sit and talk to her and encourage her to eat.

The next thing the staff knew had to be done was prepare the house for a wake to follow the funeral. Every piece of silver was polished, dishes were washed, linens ironed, and anything else they could think of to make the house perfect so Miss Peg didn't have to think about anything. She had trained them all well.

Chapter 13

Sixty-two years old is much too young to die. Patrick wasn't ready to retire. His death would cause a shake-up at the plant. James was only twenty-two years old, just fresh out of college. He had spent very little time with Patrick learning the business. He did expect to take over his father's seat as CEO and President of Martin Metal. Instead of mourning his father's death, he was making waves at the plant trying to take over. For as much as they didn't want to, the Board of Directors contacted Miss Peg to shut down James' actions.

The staff had never seen Miss Peg angry. Her anger now though was more than they could comprehend. James came home from the plant just fuming because no one would allow him to look at any of the operational books. That information was confidential, understandably. He just wanted to see mostly what he would make as the CEO and President—a position he figured he had a right to take over.

To say she was livid was putting it mildly. She really lit into James when he got home. She was in no mood for his disrespect, and certainly wouldn't tolerate it.

Miss Peg: "Just what did you expect to accomplish by going to the plant? Did you really think they would just hand this all over to you? Your father just died; have you no respect or sadness? You have no right to anything right now."

James: "That's where you are wrong, Mother. I have a right to all of it because I *am* a Martin. Father would have wanted it this way. I know he wanted me to take over someday. At his age he was probably ready to retire anyway."

Miss Peg: "That's where you are very wrong. He wasn't ready to retire. I don't know what brought on this heavy drinking but it wasn't because he was retiring. You have no clue as to what it takes to run our company. I doubt you've spent more than a couple of hours there. You haven't even tried to learn the business. Do you think I was just going to hand it over to you? Your father worked too hard to build that company, just to have you destroy it. Right now I'm the major shareholder. The Board of Directors answers to me. You have shown me by this stunt that you should never be in charge of anything. Your disrespect for your father has made me all the more determined."

James just looked at Miss Peg with anger in his eyes.

"I don't have time for your nonsense right now. I have your father's funeral to put together. I suggest you get your act together so no one else catches wind of your actions. Instead of trying to take over you need to sit down and write a heartfelt eulogy."

"Oh—and by the way, your money tree just withered. If you aren't working there will be no money put in your account. Your days of being spoiled are over."

James stormed out of Miss Peg's office grumbling and slamming any door he had to go through. Instead of a gold mine, he got a coal mine.

Laura walked in to check on Miss Peg just as James stormed out past her.

James: "Out of my way, Dogpatch. You are the last person I want to see today."

She had no idea what had set him off. She just side-stepped him as he stormed by. He obviously didn't get his way on something. She doubted his mood had anything to do with the sorrow of his father's death. That kind of compassion wasn't his nature. Oh well, it would work itself out she figured. Her main concern was helping Miss Peg get through this like Miss Peg helped her get through the death of both her parents. That was priority one.

Laura: "Miss Peg, are you all right? James looked pretty angry when he came out of here."

Miss Peg: "Yes, I am as fine as to be expected. James just isn't happy about what will go on at the plant. He won't take over like he assumed he would. His father had no intention of just handing it over to him. This will only be his first temper tantrum. When the will is read he will explode. We'll cross that bridge when we come to it though."

Patrick Martin, 62,
died Monday, November 10, 2004 after a short illness.

He was born April 17, 1942 in Kester to Michael and Madelaine(Steinman) Martin both of whom preceded him in death.

He married Margaret Banks January 13, 1980. She survives along with a son, James.

He has been the owner of Martin Metal Fabrication for the last 25 years serving as CEO and President at the time of his death.

Patrick was a long standing member of the local Elks Lodge where he enjoyed an occasional round of golf with other members.

Patrick started scholarship funds in each of Kester's high schools for students looking to further their education in Math or Engineering.

He was respected by industry leaders around the world whom he associated with through his company. He hosted many foreign industry leaders to encourage them to buy products made in the USA.

Viewing will be Sunday November 16, 2004 from 3 p.m. to 7p.m. at McCullough Memorial Chapel and at 10 a.m. November 17, 2004 before Graveside Services at 11 a.m. at Grace Serenity Gardens where he will be interred in the family mausoleum.

The entire three shifts at the plant were closed down with pay on the day of Patrick's funeral. This gave anyone who cared to attend, the chance to. There were a lot at the viewing but that was it.

The activity at the Martin household was hectic for the next week. Since Martin Metal had so many suppliers and product purchasers, Patrick's funeral couldn't be a quick affair. The Board of Directors had to contact all of them about Patrick's passing. There were phone calls with follow-up letters. All of these businesses needed the assurance that it would be business as usual. At any given time they had dealings with everyone on the board so they were comfortable knowing one of them would take over. The chain of command had just shifted.

Two people were quickly elected to the board to replace Patrick. Miss Peg and the board decided that one person should not be CEO and president. Patrick held both positions but that's because of the fact that he was the company owner so he decided that was how it should be. Two current board members were voted to hold those positions. A woman from the office pool was voted in to fill the vacant seat on the board. James wasn't included in any of the decisions. His anger was palpable. His position with the company remained as assistant manager of exports. Patrick would probably have elevated his position but Miss Peg wouldn't. She felt he didn't deserve anything he didn't earn even if his last name was Martin.

Miss Peg was right about how angry James would be when he heard what was in the will. Miss Peg was given total control of everything. The company and all its properties were to be used at her discretion. James got his father's car and $500 a month over his salary at the plant until he turned thirty. After that, the extra money stopped. It looked as though Patrick felt he would have made something of himself by then.

According to Miss Peg he really exploded at the attorney's office. James' money scheme that he held over his father's head came to a screeching halt.

Chapter 14

The September before Patrick died Elizabeth and Jeremiah started their sophomore year in high school. They were now eligible to work on dual credits toward college. Every day after leaving high school they both worked on one of the two classes at the college level.

Laura worried that this would put a lot of undue pressure on them. They were determined though. David, Sharon and now Laura had been putting money aside so they could go to college to pursue their careers. They had the simple classes they could take in high school under control. The real money would be needed for the necessary college and post-graduate studies. They both wanted Laura to start living her own life and not work extra hard to save the money for them. They hoped she would be able to go back and finish her college ambition.

As it stood Laura was doing the same three jobs, and then some that Sharon had been doing. She worked full-time as house manager for Miss Peg. She left there and cleaned a house every day during the week. At night she still did the laundry for five different people.

This is what her parents would be doing to guarantee the money was there for the twins' education. Her parents' expectations for the twins were high. She wasn't about to lower them.

Speaking of Laura living her own life...she really didn't know what that would be. She went out on one date in high school. When the boy found out he couldn't get past first base he never called again. He made sure all the other boys knew that fact, too. No one else ever asked her out. In her one year of college she was too focused on her grades to even notice anyone around her. Here she was now, twenty-two, and never been kissed.

It didn't matter. The twins were her life now and she had no problem with that. Once they were out of school and on their own she would decide where her life should go.

Chapter 15

Times at the Martins' home had gotten pretty tense since Patrick died. James was angry most of the time. The only happiness he had was when he had money in his pocket.

The one time of year he enjoyed most was when the annual Gala was about to happen. His expected date was Trinity Baker. Taking anyone else would almost be a sacrilege.

Even though James enjoyed teasing and bullying Laura he couldn't ignore the fact that she had grown to be a very attractive woman. Laura worked very hard at all her jobs so stayed very slim. She kept her hair long but tied back most of the time she worked. Her complexion only became more radiant as she got older. This allowed her sea-blue eyes to shine through all the more. This is the one thing James couldn't ignore…those beautiful blue eyes.

He thought maybe he would ask her if she would want to go to the Gala, not as his date but just go to "see how the other half lived" so to speak. Miss Peg still went once in a while. She could "drag" Laura with her. He'd have to bring it up when he saw his mother. Who knows, it might be a kick.

James did bring it up to Miss Peg. She knew her son. He had an ulterior motive she was sure. Considering the way he had treated her she was not about to put Laura through that.

Miss Peg: "You're my son and I love you but I'll be honest, she's too good for you. Don't even think about bringing it up to her. Considering the way you and your friends treat her I wouldn't put it past any of you to do something to humiliate her."

James: "It would take too much to make her presentable anyway. I doubt she owns anything besides jeans or her uniform. I'll pass on it this year. Maybe between this year, and next year, you can make her more presentable."

Miss Peg just shook her head and walked away. She could not for the life of her understand how his personality changed so much.

Chapter 16

The years just started to slip by. Elizabeth and Jeremiah were doing exceptionally well in school. This was the year they needed to start applying for colleges. There seemed to be more than they realized. Right now they couldn't imagine not being here with Laura. Most of their education wasn't available in Kester.

The culinary school Jeremiah wanted to attend for the best studies was in Chicago. That was at least a five-hour drive from Kester. He couldn't do that daily so would have to stay in a dorm.

It was the same situation with Elizabeth. She could get her bachelor's degree locally but to go on for her master's and PA degree would mean traveling a ways away.

Right now those thoughts were ones neither wanted to think about.

As their senior year was about to come to an end they were both happier than they thought they could be. Both were going to prom with someone special. The prom for the twins' high school this year was being held in the ballroom at the Martin Estate. Miss Peg had followed how the Parker twins had been doing since the death of their mother. Laura was always bragging about how well they were doing in school. Miss Peg thought she would do something special for them.

The staff and hired help went all out to make the ballroom very bright and festive. Balloons, streamers and flowers covered every inch that wasn't the stage or dance floor. All the students were resplendent in their formal gowns and tuxedos. Elizabeth was with Carl Nance, a boy she had been dating for the last year. Jeremiah was with Georgette Summers, his steady girlfriend since junior year. The night was magic. Laura hadn't seen the twins this happy in years. She watched them thinking they deserved this after all they had been through. Her parents would have loved this.

The wonderful part for Laura was that they were both graduating with honors. This time next year they would be well on their way to their respective careers. Her parents would be so proud of how they were doing. Nothing could put a damper on their lives right now.

Chapter 17

Another year, another annual Gala. This year though James did say something to Laura about attending the Gala. She just laughed.

Laura: "To be honest, Jim, that is one thing I have never wanted to do. I didn't even go to my senior prom in high school. In case you haven't noticed I'm a little more down to earth than that. I could never justify spending a lot of money on a gown to be worn once. I relented though when my sister wanted to go to her prom. We've been denied enough these last years. I'll do anything to bring joy to their lives. It just isn't for me. Besides...why would I subject myself to all your friends in one place all at once? Especially in a place where they are the most comfortable...a very expensive gathering. What? Do you all have some sort of prank you're planning to play on me to make me look ridiculous? No thanks. Go have a good time."

James: "Your loss."

James was disappointed that Laura wasn't going to the Gala. He did have something planned to humiliate her but now had to put the thought on the back burner.

Laura didn't have an expensive gown, so she would have to either buy or rent one. Missy Perkins who would be going with Matt Roman would loan her one. That would be humiliation one, wearing a gown already seen by everyone. Number two would be they all would pour part of their drinks on the back of her gown without her knowledge. She would walk around the Gala with a ruined gown and not even know it. It would have been perfect in James' eyes.

Chapter 18

Miss Peg was having a garden party this year. She wanted to do something happy. Patrick's death seemed to make the entire household dark once all the prom decorations had been removed. The planning had been going on for weeks. This last week the entire house was turned inside out to be cleaned. Everything sparkled, or shined, or had been pressed to within an inch of its life. Laura was very proud of how it was all coming together. She decided to go see Miss Peg on Sunday, her normal day off, to help her decide what china she thought she should use.

The party had a Victorian theme so Laura thought she found just the right china pattern to use. Everything had been planned to the smallest detail right down to the uniforms the staff and extra hired staff would wear.

The party would be held in Miss Peg's rose garden. At this time of year, barely two weeks from now, the peonies and roses would be in full bloom. The fragrances were amazing when all the different flowers and colors were popping.

Charles worked with a local gardener to make sure everything was pruned properly. The block patio was scrubbed. If, by some slim chance, it rained that day all the tents had been brought out and opened to air them out. They were taking no chances that this wouldn't turn out perfectly.

Charles had been with the Martin family for over twenty years. He was tall and thin with graying hair. He had an air about him that just let you know he was in charge. There wasn't a thing that he couldn't fix.

Laura and Miss Peg were in the sitting room enjoying some tea and pleasant conversation. They had become more than employer/employee over the years. They enjoyed each other's company. The years between them didn't matter.

They were both looking forward to seeing all the ladies in their Victorian-era gowns and hats. It would be very exhilarating. It would be the social event of the year not counting the annual Gala that was held last night.

Laura: "What kind of condition was James in when he got home last night?"

Miss Peg: "He hasn't come home yet. That isn't surprising though. I think Trinity is wrangling for a wedding ring. She's been very attentive lately. She probably thinks James will still come into a lot of money when I die and she wants some of it. I'm afraid they're both in for a rude awakening."

Chapter 19

James walked in the door. His tuxedo was all wrinkled, his shirt open, and hair messed up, unlike his normal clean-cut look. He must have really done a lot of drinking last night because you could still smell it on him. If truth be told, he was probably still very drunk.

James: "Hello, Mother. Damn, it's Sunday afternoon. Why do I have to look at you, Dogpatch?"

Miss Peg: "James, that is enough. You're still drunk I won't have you talking like that."

James: "Fine. It would have been better though if I didn't have to see her so much."

Laura: "I have yet to figure out why you feel you need to treat me the way you do. I have always been nice to you, well, almost. There was the day after my mother died but you had that coming. You and your friends tease and try to humiliate me all the time I just want to know why."

James just stood there for a minute or so trying to put it together. When he did answer it was like a bomb went off in the room.

James: "Because your family killed my father which left me almost penniless. Until I get back what is due me, I'll continue treating you like you don't matter because you don't."

Laura: "Now wait a minute. Are you nuts? There is no way that is possible. My father worked at your father's company and my mom and I have worked here. That's as close as it goes. Your father drank himself to death. My family had nothing to do with that. You act like we poured the bourbon down his throat. That was all his doing. If I remember correctly, he didn't need any help there. So your assertion that we had anything to do with your father's death is way off base. Sounds like you need someone to blame besides your father."

James just stood there contemplating whether to go any further. He was drunk enough though that his tongue had already loosened up. He may as well keep going. What harm would it do?

James: "My father drank himself to death out of guilt. Unfortunately he had a conscience and had done something he was having trouble dealing with, when he was sober."

Laura: "You're blaming my family for your dad's guilt about something *he* did?"

James: "Yes, I am."

Miss Peg: "James, what did he do? Quit beating around the bush and explain yourself...NOW!"

James still had trouble saying out loud what had happened. Even years after his death he was still trying to protect Patrick. He had already said too much but didn't know how to stop now.

James: "Dad was the hit and run driver that killed Laura's dad."

Miss Peg and Laura gasped.

It felt as though all the air had been sucked out of the room. Miss Peg just stood there staring at James.

Laura fell back into a chair as if she had been hit in the chest.

No one spoke. The thought of what James just said was too hard to imagine. After several minutes of what James said sank in, Laura could just look at him. She didn't want to believe him but it would make perfect sense.

Laura: "How do you know this?"

James: "Dad told me."

Miss Peg: "When did he tell you this?"

James: "A little over a year after it happened."

Laura was up and pacing by now. Her head was spinning. James had known this for all of these years and never said a word.

Laura: "Why would your dad just tell you that? What made him confess to you?"

James: "It wasn't something he just volunteered. Trinity and I thought we would go skinny dipping in the pond after school was out. I remembered that there were always towels in the boat shed. When I opened the door I found Dad's car...his silver Mercedes. There was a lot of damage to the front end. I wondered what had happened to that car. About a year earlier Dad started driving a black Mercedes. At the time I figured he just wanted a new car. He did change cars often. Then I remembered about your dad's accident and put two and two together."

Laura just paced the floor faster.

"I closed the door and told Trinity there weren't any towels in there. She knew I wouldn't want any wet clothes on my car seats so didn't grumble when we just left."

"After I took Trinity home I returned and told Dad I found his old car. I asked him what was his wrecked car doing in the boat shed and how did he wreck it? Why didn't he just get it fixed? He didn't answer me right away. His face just went pale. It took him a few minutes to actually answer me."

Miss Peg: "I remember when he got that new car. He told me he sold the other one and got a new one. I never questioned his explanation."

Laura: "Keep going. What was his explanation for the damage to his car?"

James sat down and put his head in his hands. The explanation did not come easily.

James: "Dad said he was coming home from a board meeting. Everyone, especially him, was drinking pretty heavily. As he turned onto Broadway the sun hit his eyes just right...blinding him. Before he knew what had happened he felt he had hit something. He looked up in time to see someone moving through the air. He realized he had hit someone on a bike. He panicked and drove away. When he got here he just pulled the car into the boat shed and walked to the house. He called his friend at the dealership and had him deliver a new vehicle here first thing in the morning. He found out on the news that night that he had actually hit and killed your dad. He obviously didn't know who you were then. He knew he would probably go to jail, and he couldn't imagine that so he never said anything."

'The police were looking for a silver car so he knew his car should just rot in the boat shed until he figured out what to do with it. That's how I found it—rotting in the boat shed. Now do you see? Leaving me his car in his will was like a slap in the face or a final 'GOTCHA.'"

"I figured I might as well get something for not saying anything. For my silence, I got whatever I wanted for at least the last three or so years before he died. Toward the end he must have thought I might still say something so his drinking got heavier."

Miss Peg and Laura couldn't believe what they had just heard. The pain James' silence had caused was unbelievable. Miss Peg couldn't believe either Patrick or James could be so callous about another person's life.

Laura was in shock. All these years there was no word about her father's death. What hurt the most was that she had taken care of the man who had killed her father. James certainly wasn't innocent in all of this either. He witnessed how all of this affected Laura and her family and just didn't seem to care. What was worse was that he blamed her father for Patrick's death when actually it was the other way around. For the second time in her life she felt anger like she had never felt before.

She jumped up from her chair and literally attacked James. This time it was with both fists. She wasn't strong enough to do any damage but she needed to try anyway. Miss Peg came up to her and wrapped her arms around her to try and calm her down.

With a calmer head, Laura confronted James.

Laura: "You know, Jim, if your father had turned himself in he probably would still be alive today. He was a prominent figure in town. He may have gone to a country club prison to serve out his time if he went at all. And you know what? He wouldn't have died from his drinking. You would still have all the money you could talk out of him. See, you shot yourself in the foot with that one. And if you want to look at it differently— you killed your father by not turning him in."

"The way I see it you also killed my mother. She never got over losing my dad. She just withered away. I blame you for both."

Miss Peg: "James, go get out of those clothes and take a shower. I can't stand the smell of the alcohol on you. We will deal with this later. Laura, please sit down. I'll fix this…I promise."

James left the room and Laura really broke down into tears. Miss Peg just held her.

While this was going on, Benjamin came in. It was a coincidence that he had come over to show her the budget for the garden party before going to the bank on Monday morning.

Miss Peg: "Hello, Benjamin. Why are you here?"

Benjamin: "Bringing you the numbers for your party. What is going on? Laura, are you okay?"

Miss Peg: "I'll explain all in a bit. I need you to make a phone call for me first. I need you to call Sheriff Stone and tell him I need him out here right away. Tell him it isn't an emergency so no lights and sirens, but I need him out here. It's something that can't wait. Do that for me, please, while I sit with Laura, then I'll explain everything. I'm glad you're here. We'll need your help."

"Laura, listen to me. James will not get away with not saying something all of these years. He's just as guilty as Patrick. His motive was more despicable. He did it to blackmail his father for his silence. I think he's probably just as responsible. We'll find out the legalities from the Sheriff when he gets here."

Benjamin: "I talked to the Sheriff. He'll be here as soon as he can get here. He's all the way across town so it'll be thirty to forty-five minutes. Now can you tell me why we need the Sheriff out here? Laura, are you hurt, or did someone do something to you?"

Laura: "Physically I'm fine. I feel like I want to puke right now but I'm okay. My goodness, Miss Peg, how will I explain this to the twins? After all these years..."

Miss Peg: "We'll cross that bridge in a bit. You can't change anything about what happened so let's fix what we can now—okay?"

Miss Peg quickly explained to Benjamin what had transpired. He was just as shocked as they were. He had no clue.

Miss Peg: "Benjamin, I need you to do something for me before the Sheriff gets here. For right now you need to keep the results under your hat."

Benjamin: "You know I'll do anything that I can for you, Miss Peg. What is it?"

Miss Peg: "I need you to go down to the boat shed and see what is in there. I think I know what is there. I need you to tell me out of earshot if the Sheriff is here. If he is here shake your head 'yes' or 'no.' You'll understand when you find out the answer."

Benjamin: "I can probably get there and back before the Sheriff gets here.... Be right back."

Miss Peg: "Laura, if the car is there I'm going to have the Sheriff go and see if it is the car he's been looking for all these years. I have a feeling James will be in hot water."

Laura: "He can't just go in there, I don't think, even with your permission. For it to be a legal search he may need a search warrant. You're going to have to give him a reason for the search. If for some reason Jim has broken the law, his attorney will fight any unauthorized search. You need to think this through. This could get sticky."

Within minutes Benjamin was back with a look of shock on his face.

Benjamin: "There is an older wrecked silver Mercedes in the boat shed. Was that Mr. Patrick's car? What is it doing there? James was right, wasn't he? This is not good. What are you going to do?"

Miss Peg: "At this point I'm not sure. I need to ask the Sheriff to see where we stand. I don't know the law but I can venture a guess that James could be in some real trouble by keeping this all to himself all of these years. Laura, I told you I would fix this. Do you trust me to do the right thing? I'm the one that called the Sheriff, not you, so you can't be blamed for the outcome of this. Are you okay with this?"

Benjamin: "Miss Peg, I need to ask. Do you think you should call an attorney for James?"

Miss Peg: "I will dance around the questions with the Sheriff. Obviously we don't have a criminal attorney. Our attorney, Sam Lancaster, is on a cruise in the Bahamas so he couldn't be here anyway, not that he would want to. James will expect me to get him an attorney and pay for it but I'm stepping away from this. This is all on James. Let's wait and see what the Sheriff has to say. James will have to be arrested anyway before he'll need an attorney."

Laura: "Yes, I'm okay with all of this. Just because you called the Sheriff gives me a feeling of trust. I know you'll do the right thing. I need to be here when the Sheriff gets here but will let you handle it. I won't say anything unless he asks me. I'm still in shock by all of this anyway."All these years, and he treated me like it was my fault about Patrick. He has been angry at the wrong person all this time. I was just his scapegoat, I guess. You know what else this means don't you? I really can't in good conscience continue to work here. It isn't your fault but I don't think the twins would forgive me for working for the family that killed our parents."

Miss Peg: "That *is* unfortunate. I suppose you are right though. We have a lot of things to work out. This will get messy, that is for sure.

Chapter 20

True to his word, within forty-five minutes of Benjamin's call, Sheriff Stone pulled into the Martins' driveway.

Sheriff Stone was a big man, definitely not one you would want to wrestle with. Too many sweets though would probably keep him from chasing anyone for much of a distance. His ruddy complexion reflected his many hours outside doing a job not too many people would want to do. He was also a fair and honest man. He followed the law to the letter. The situation at the Martins' home would definitely put that to a test.

Miss Peg answered the door and showed him into the drawing room. Benjamin and Laura were there holding a quiet conversation.

Miss Peg: "Sheriff, can I get you something to drink? Tea, coffee? I assume you're on duty so something stronger is out of the question."

Sheriff Stone: "I'd love a glass of your sweet tea. Thank you. I know it to be the best in the county."

Laura got up but Miss Peg signaled for her to stay put.

Sheriff: "Miss Parker, I was at the commencement. My boy, Billy, graduated this year along with your twins. Their commencement speeches were well thought out and inspirational. They will go far thinking the way they do."

Laura: "Thank you, Sheriff. I'm very proud of them. These last four years haven't been easy on them but they've worked very hard. They'll both be going to Central Illinois University for two years to finish their bachelor's degrees and then go on to post graduate. Jeremiah has just one more year after that of culinary school then he may study in France right after that. Elizabeth had her two years of nursing then her master's then off to medical school. They have both been very focused."

Sheriff: "I'm sure your parents would have been extremely proud of them."

Laura: "Yes, I know they would. This is what we've all worked toward."

Miss Peg came back with the tea. Once everyone was settled Sheriff Stone started the conversation.

Sheriff: "So, Miss Peg, I know you didn't call me over for some of your tea. By the way, my wife is looking forward to your garden party. She's been working on her gown since she received her invitation. But what is going on that you felt I needed to come out right away? I don't see Jim. Is he or someone else hurt?"

Miss Peg: "I'm not sure where to start. None of this will be pleasant."

"We will help you close a cold case today if you want to work on it. It will probably require a search warrant and an arrest warrant before the day is over. Explain to me first, what are the requirements to obtain a search warrant."

Sheriff: "You need strong probable cause to get one. Someone or something needs to point to the area to be searched. Law enforcement can't just go in somewhere because they think there is something there they may want. The one way around a search warrant is if the person in control of the area gives law enforcement permission to search. A lot of defense lawyers find some sneaky ways around that way though. The safest to make sure the evidence is found is with a judge-signed search warrant. The lawyer can still try to get around that search but usually fails."

Laura: "Okay, let me be clear on this. Hypothetically, let's say you think there might be a gun in, say, the credenza over there. You know it's there but can't just walk over there and get it without a warrant. But, if Miss Peg permits you to search it, that gun can be used as evidence."

Sheriff: "Yes, that's right."

Laura: "Now I told you the gun is in there but Miss Peg isn't crazy about you digging through her linens and told you to get a warrant. Is my say-so that the gun is in there enough probable cause for you to get the warrant?"

Sheriff: "Did you see the gun in there?"

Laura: "Yes, I did."

Sheriff: "You are a credible witness so I would take that statement to a judge...warrant in hand. Nine out of ten times the Judge will sign the warrant on my word that you are a credible witness. You have my interest piqued. Who is going to tell me where the gun is hidden?"

Laura: "Miss Peg, should I go on or should you?"

Miss Peg: "I'll take over. Your questions helped me make up my mind.

"Sheriff, we found out today that it was my husband, Patrick, who was the hit-and-run driver that killed Laura's father. The story could all be hearsay but we doubt it. The explanation of how and when it happened all makes sense."

The look on the Sheriff's face indicated he was surprised but not shocked by the revelation.

Sheriff: "Patrick is dead though. He can't be prosecuted. Who gave you all this information?"

Miss Peg: "James told us that Patrick told him how it all occurred."

Sheriff: "What is the reason for a search warrant. Does James have a recording of Patrick confessing to him?"

Benjamin: "My turn. No, Sheriff. He led us to the car."

Sheriff: "The luxury silver car....I wondered about that when it happened. Considering where it happened the thought that it could be someone from the plant crossed my mind. So why a search warrant since Patrick can't be charged?"

Miss Peg was wrestling with this considering what she had to do about it.

Miss Peg: "No, but I think James can be charged. He has known about all of it since right after it happened. For his silence Patrick spoiled James. He gave him anything he wanted. Once Patrick died though all his perks stopped. He has gotten angrier and angrier over these past years. He came home this morning and saw Laura here so he exploded and let it all out."

"He told us how it happened...word for word the way Patrick told him...and where the car is. It pains me to turn my son in but he kept all this all these years. He's made life miserable for the wrong people. I know there are a couple things he can be charged with. I love my son but can't excuse him for the hateful things he has done...especially since Patrick died. The main reason I'm doing this is that Laura and her family have a right to get closure on how their father was killed. James has known but only tormented this family over all these years. What is our next move?"

Sheriff: "First—who has actually seen the car?"

Benjamin: "Me."

Sheriff: "So it's somewhere close?"

Benjamin: "Yes, very close."

Sheriff: "On this property?"

Benjamin: "Yes."

Sheriff: "Let me go make a phone call then I'll let you know what I'll have to do next. And, Miss Peg, if this search does turn up the car you were right about James. He was responsible for his part in covering all this. After the car, I may need to arrest James. You probably shouldn't say anything to him right now."

Miss Peg: "No problem. I'll have to wake him up to tell him. I see no reason to do that."

Sheriff Stone went outside to make his phone calls. He was out there for a while. When he came back in he had the answers that he needed.

Sheriff: "I talked to the Prosecutor and explained all of this to him. He told me how to word the search warrant and he would take it to a judge to sign it as soon as I got it to him. I called my deputy and told him what the Prosecutor said. I'm going back to the office and getting the warrant to the Prosecutor. There is one thing. Do I search your whole property or is there a specific area we should look? Like, say, all the outbuildings?"

Benjamin: "I would say outbuildings. If there was something here close to the house we would have probably discovered it before now."

Sheriff: "Miss Peg, Miss Parker, I'm sorry to put you through all this but I'm sure you'll be glad it's over. If we find what I think we may find there may be an arrest yet today. I'll keep this as low-key as possible. We don't need a bunch of looky-loos nosing around."

Miss Peg: "Thank you, Sheriff. I know I can count on you using as much discretion as possible."

With that Sheriff Stone left. Miss Peg, Laura, and Benjamin just sat without talking for a long time.

Laura couldn't believe how all of this had happened. She knew she needed to tell Elizabeth and Jeremiah but was still wondering how to tell them. She knew she needed to tell them in person but didn't want to leave yet. She wanted to be here when the car was found and James was arrested. The Sheriff didn't or couldn't give them a time frame when all of this would happen so she was torn. Should she wait to tell them until after they found the car or tell them before?

She decided to call them and have them at home to tell them before the search. Seeing the car would probably be traumatic for all three of them but they weren't kids anymore. They had suffered through the worst of it. They had the right to be here for the conclusion. She'd let them decide if they wanted to see the car get revealed.

Chapter 21

When Laura got home Elizabeth was already there.

Laura: "Do you know where Jeremiah is? I need him to come home. I have something to tell the both of you."

Elizabeth: "I think he's at the park with his buddies playing basketball. Laura, what's wrong? Tell me."

Laura; "Let me get Jeremiah home then I'll explain."

Laura called Jeremiah and he said he'd be right home.

When Jeremiah did get home Laura sat them down. This wouldn't be an easy conversation.

Laura: "I went to see Miss Peg this afternoon to work on her garden party. While we sat there James came home—drunk—which isn't unusual for him. He must have really tied one on last night at the annual Gala. He's never happier than when he's with his rich friends and showing off. Anyway, when he saw me sitting there he really went off on me again. If you can believe this...he blames us for his father's death."

Laura was starting to get visibly shaken. She needed to get to the truth of why she had the kids come home.

Jeremiah: "I knew that guy was nuts. Everyone knows Patrick Martin drank himself to death. How are we even remotely responsible?"

Laura: "His anger and nasty behavior are due to his father's death but, you're right, he's nuts. Let me finish this while I still can. Here's the tricky part. He told me and Miss Peg that (sigh) Patrick was the driver who hit and killed Dad."

Elizabeth: "WHAT??!! How was that possible? James has known that all this time? How can anyone be so cruel?"

Jeremiah: "Man!! You know I'm not the kind to hurt anyone but I want to beat the crap out of him right now!"

Laura: "Okay, hold on. Actually I punched him myself but that isn't what we're going to do right now. Here's how stupid both James and Patrick were. The car Patrick was driving is still on their property. Patrick never got rid of it. After James spilled his guts to us, Miss Peg called Sheriff Stone. To be sure the car was still there, Miss Peg sent Benjamin to check. When the Sheriff got there we explained to him what had gone on that afternoon. There's so much to explain but not right now. Sheriff Stone is in the process right now of obtaining a search warrant to search the outbuildings on the Martin property for the car. According to James there is a lot of damage on the front end. Oh, by the way, it is a silver Mercedes."

"As soon as the Sheriff finds the car he said he would probably arrest James. What I want to know is if you want to be there when they find the car and arrest James? Seeing the car could be very upsetting. It'll be hard to see what kind of damage a human body and bike can do to a car. We already know what the car did to Dad."

"All these years James treated me like dirt because his dad drank out of guilt for killing our father. He's been mad because when Patrick died, Miss Peg pulled the plug on his bottomless bank account. He was blackmailing his father to get anything he wanted, from trips, to new cars, and all the money he could spend. All to not say anything. Pretty sad, really. Patrick was probably afraid James would still turn him in after James found the car so he gave in to all of James' demands."

"Essentially I came home to tell you what was going on. You aren't little kids anymore. You should be involved in anything that goes on when it comes to this. Seeing all of this could be...well...traumatic. I don't want to put you both through anything unnecessary. I've tried to protect you from all I could since both Dad and Mom died. No one should have to go through what we've all gone through the last almost eight years. What happens today will be the beginning to the end of this nightmare."

"Do you want to go out there? You don't have to. If you do we need to go soon. Once the Sheriff gets there to serve the search warrant it'll be blocked off. The Sheriff said he'll try and keep the whole thing kinda quiet so as not to disrupt anything for Miss Peg, if he can. When they find the car though they'll have a tow truck to remove it. After that James will probably be arrested. There will be so much commotion that it'll be hard to keep it all quiet. I feel bad for Miss Peg right now. She did what she thought was right—something no parent should have to do—turn her child in to the police."

The twins just sat there and stared.

"Oh, by the way, I quit my job for Miss Peg. I wouldn't be comfortable working for the family that killed our dad. That's too bad, too. I was actually enjoying myself there. Miss Peg and I have become great friends over the years. I'll miss that."

"Okay, if we're going to go I guess we should leave. Decide...do you want to go or stay here?"

In unison both Elizabeth and Jeremiah said: "We're going!"

Chapter 22

When Laura and the twins got to the Martins' estate the Sheriff hadn't gotten back yet. They went right in to see Miss Peg. No one knew what would happen yet.

About thirty minutes after they got to the Martins' home, the Sheriff returned. There were three other deputies with him. Sheriff Stone came to the house with one deputy, while the other two deputies started looking through the outbuildings. There are were greenhouses, barns, potting sheds, the boat house, and two garages.

Sheriff Stone: "Mrs. Martin, I'm here to serve a search warrant for all your outbuildings. We are searching for any and all evidence pertaining to the hit-and-run death of David Parker. If you know where any evidence may be now would be the time to tell me."

Miss Peg: "Hmm, I didn't know that was an option. You might want to start with the boat shed. It will probably save your deputies some time."

Sheriff: "Thank you, Mrs. Martin, that is helpful. I have also spoken to the Prosecutor. Is your son, James, at home?"

Miss Peg: "Yes, he is up in his room."

Sheriff: "Could you direct us to that room, please?"

Miss Peg: "Follow me."

Miss Peg, Sheriff Stone, and the deputy went to James' room on the second floor. Miss Peg knocked.

Miss Peg: "James, are you awake? May I come in?"

James: (Groggily) "Yes, Mother, I am. What do you want? I don't want to talk right now. I have one helluva hangover. Go away."

Sheriff Stone opened the door and walked in.

Sheriff: "James Martin, get up. You are under arrest for Obstruction of Justice and Accessory After the Fact of the Second Degree Vehicular Manslaughter of David Parker. Get dressed. NOW! Deputy get him a shirt and then cuff him."

The Sheriff tossed a pair of pants that were laying on the floor to James to put on.

James: "What the hell? Mother, what is going on? Is Laura responsible for this? I'll get back at her. If she thinks I've harassed her before just wait until I get out of jail."

Sheriff: "Be careful what you say, James. That could come back and bite you. I'm going to read you your rights."

"You have the right to remain silent. Anything you say can and will be used against you in a court of law. You have the right to an attorney. If you cannot afford an attorney, one will be provided for you."

"Do you understand these rights as I have said them to you?"

James: "Yes, I hear you."

Miss Peg: "Laura had nothing to do with the police. I called them. I can't believe you've kept this to yourself all of these years. To top it off you have tormented Laura for no reason at all. Someone needs to pay for her father's death. You should have let Patrick admit to it."

Just as the four of them were getting downstairs one of the deputies walked in.

Deputy: "Sheriff, we found a silver Mercedes with significant right front end damage in the boat shed. I've called for a tow truck to come and get it. The car is pretty dirty. Looks like it's been in there for a while. Interesting fact: a closed up car maintains the old smells in it. When we opened the driver's door there was a strong smell of alcohol. The keys are still in the ignition."

Sheriff: "Thanks, Deputy Friend. You two, take Mr. Martin and book him. I'll stay here and wait for the tow. I'm also going to get a statement from Mrs. Martin."

James did not go out to the deputy's car easily. He was struggling, still screaming and cursing.

Sheriff Stone walked into the drawing room with Miss Peg. Laura, Elizabeth, Jeremiah and Benjamin were there waiting for them. Miss Peg was shaking from the previous incident with James. She didn't expect to be so upset to see him get arrested. It was Laura's turn to comfort her. She sat her down and put her arms around her.

The Sheriff sat down in a chair and faced the five people.

Sheriff: "Do any of you mind if I record your statements? I can have a stenographer type it up. You can then sign it. It'll save you from having to go down to the police station. It can be pretty intimidating there."

Everyone agreed. After about an hour and a half, Miss Peg, Laura, and Benjamin had told the Sheriff the same thing James had told them. This was the first time Elizabeth and Jeremiah heard the entire story. They sat there quietly. The look of pain and disbelief on their faces was saddening. They held on to each other tightly the entire time. This was the part Laura knew they needed to hear but was dreading. They were young when it happened but remembered how they felt. It hit hard now when they heard all the horrible details. Unfortunately it wouldn't be for the last time. They'd hear it again at James' trial.

Sheriff: "Miss Peg, I'm sorry to have had to put you through that. I'm sure watching the arrest of your only child was upsetting. When I spoke to the Prosecutor to get the search warrant I explained all the circumstances. He told me that whether or not we found the car he wanted James arrested. He felt the car was just extra. James' actions were what he was interested in pursuing. He remembered the accident. He wanted to see this case concluded. I need to go supervise removing the car. I'm sure you want all of us out of here. Miss Parker, Elizabeth, and Jeremiah, I hope this brings the closure you need and deserve. None of this can be easy. I'm sorry it had to take so long. I wish your mother could have seen it happen. I remember how difficult it was for her."

"Once the press gets hold of this it'll be a circus. If you are hounded by the media or anyone else you let me know. The same goes to you, Miss Peg. Considering your standing in the community, there will be a lot of publicity...both good and bad. If you need police protection to let you live quietly let me know. I don't want any of you harassed."

With that the Sheriff left. The tow truck had the car on the bed and was getting ready to leave. This was the first look any of them, except Benjamin, had of the car. Everyone just watched from the porch. It was all getting very real.

Miss Peg and Benjamin walked back into the house. It just dawned on her why Laura and Benjamin were even there. She turned to Benjamin…

Miss Peg: "Benjamin, will you please send out a card to everyone on the garden party guest list? Inform them that the garden party has been postponed, not canceled. I'm sure they'll understand after tomorrow. I wonder if any of them will even come here after this. There is no way right now though I feel we can have any kind of celebration."

Benjamin: "I'll get right on that. They'll be in the mail in the morning. I'm sorry, Miss Peg, that all of this has happened. Is there anything else I can do for you?"

Miss Peg: "No, thank you, Benjamin. I want to thank you for today though. You have been my rock. I'm just sorry I had to drag you into this."

Benjamin: "I wouldn't have had it any other way. I've said it before, I will do anything for you. (He chuckled) Charles is going to be mad he wasn't here."

Miss Peg: (laughing a little) "You're right about that."

She turned to look outside. The Parker children were still on the porch just holding on to one another. A month earlier they were on the porch laughing and dancing around for their prom. They were so happy. Today there were sad tears rolling down their cheeks. Unfortunately, today would be the day they remembered standing on the porch of this house...not their prom.

Chapter 23

Word did quickly get out that James Martin had been arrested and the reason for it. The tow truck with the car on the bed was seen going down the street. An ambitious reporter followed it to the police impound. The story ballooned from there. Reporters find things out that most people can't imagine.

Bailiff: "All rise. The Honorable Brandon Matthews presiding. (Pause.) Be seated."

James appeared in court on Monday morning for his arraignment. He didn't have a lawyer yet so he had a public defender, Greg Daily, represent him for this. The courtroom was full of James' friends. James pled "Not Guilty" to all counts.

Judge: "Issue on bail?"

Prosecutor Lenny Jacobs: "Your Honor, Mr. Martin has a lot of wealthy acquaintances with the ability to aid him to flee this court's jurisdiction. Due to the serious issue of the crime we request remand."

Greg Daily, Public Defender: "Your Honor, that's extreme for a mostly hearsay case. We request reasonable bail."

Judge: "Sorry, Mr. Daily, I agree with Mr. Jacobs. After all these years of freedom I'm sure Mr. Martin would rather be sitting on a beach in the Bahamas. He would probably be there before you could blink instead of sitting in jail. We'll go for an early trial. Mr. Martin, you will stay in jail until then. Court dismissed."

Chapter 24

James was back in court on Friday to be told that his trial would be Tuesday, September 11. This was the earliest date on the Judge's docket that was available. James' public defender called a friend of his to see if he wanted to represent James. Greg wasn't about to continue to defend someone with as much money as he figured James had, pro bono.

Bailiff: "All rise. The Honorable Brandon Matthews presiding. (Pause.) Be seated."

Judge: "Are there any questions or motions at this time?

Edward Bishop was representing James at the hearing. He stood up.

Edward Bishop was a short, stout man with dark hair that looked like it hadn't seen a comb in a couple days. His suit and shirt looked as if he had slept in them. The fit was also way too tight. His dark-rimmed glasses couldn't disguise the look of contempt in his eyes.

Lenny Jacobs, on the other hand, was the complete opposite of Bishop. He was tall and slim and just slightly older than Bishop. His dark blond hair was neatly combed, parted on one side. His three-piece suit was meticulously pressed as was his shirt. The expression on his face was one of intelligence and concern.

Bishop: "Yes, Your Honor. I would ask that all the charges against my client be dropped. All the evidence the Prosecutor has is coincidental and hearsay. My client was intoxicated when he told his story so much of it cannot be believed since he was under the influence."

Jacobs: "The evidence and testimony will speak for itself at trial, Your Honor. The trial should proceed."

Judge: "Defense motion denied. We will proceed with trial as planned. Next case."

Friends of James were in the courtroom and showed they weren't happy about James staying in jail that long. Derek Sanders pulled Edward Bishop aside to see if the Judge would set a bail amount this time. He figured he could get the money together if it wasn't too outrageous.

Bishop: "If it please the court, I do have one more order of business if I may."

Judge: (Sighs with exasperation.) "What is it, Mr. Bishop?"

Bishop: "I would ask that the court set some amount of bail so my client may be released. It would make defending him much easier if I had better access to him."

Prosecutor: "Your Honor, we went through this at his arraignment. The fact that one of his rich friends has just offered to pay his bail is all the more reason to keep him in jail. I do feel he would leave your jurisdiction."

Judge: "Mr. Bailey, you weren't at the arraignment. One of your colleagues represented Mr. Martin. You should have compared notes. I said no bail then; I'm saying it again now. Mr. Martin will remain in jail until his trial September 11. That is all. Next case."

Just as Miss Peg thought, James wanted her to find him a good lawyer and pay for it. She refused. What Patrick and James had done was to her, despicable. There was no recourse with Patrick but she would not hand James a "get-out-of-jail-free card." Granted, his regular paycheck stopped but he had his other ways of paying for a lawyer. He could start by having someone sell his four sports cars. Patrick had bought them all for him.

When James would get tired of a car he would just park it and buy a new one. The latest one, a Ferrari, might sell for enough to get his new lawyer's interest.

Miss Peg was tough but fair. As James was now twenty-six years old, Miss Peg was no longer paying his way. Let his assets do it.

Chapter 25

It would be at least ten weeks before the mess with James would again be in the limelight. Miss Peg had really been looking forward to her garden party. It might just be possible to have the party after James was off everyone's mind for a while. She was aware that there would be a lot of questions she'd have to answer. She was willing to do that. That way the truth would be passed around, instead of rumors.

Miss Peg: "Benjamin, will you please come in here?"

Benjamin: "What can I do for you, Miss Peg?"

Miss Peg: "The garden party is back on. Schedule it for three weeks from this Saturday. I'm not sure how most of these ladies will respond. Make sure you put a short date on for the RSVP. I think they'll show up out of curiosity just to see exactly what is going on. As a joke on the invitation we could put: 'You have questions? We have answers.' Everything will be the same, same theme, colors, location. The only thing we may need to do is definitely put up the canopies. It will be in June. We have a lot of trees but I don't think there will be sufficient enough shade. Tie all the arrangements down that you can as soon as possible. I'll go have a meeting with the staff and let them know it's back on so they can start to prepare again for one great party."

Benjamin turns to leave.

"I do need to talk to Laura. I think she had some ideas on china and linens. I have missed her terribly this week. I should have been able to talk to her like I do you. We had become friends, and I miss that. Maybe she'll help with this anyway. I will pay her, of course. I know she could use the income and added distraction. I'll have to work on it."

Laura did agree to help finish putting all the final details together. She had looked forward to the party as much as Miss Peg did. She was glad to finish what she had started.

Chapter 26

The day of the party turned out perfect. Temps were in the mid 70s with a slight breeze. The canopies were put up. They were needed, just as Miss Peg thought. The added shade was welcomed.

The attendance was impressive. Miss Peg wasn't sure some of the women would show because of the scandal with James, even though they said they would. Now she knew there would undoubtedly be many questions.

All the women were dressed beautifully in their Victorian-era gowns: blues, pinks, yellows, lavender, green, silks and taffetas. There were dresses with bustles. Those were taken into consideration when choosing chairs. Large dresses and small chairs don't mix.

The maids actually looked very cute in their short black dresses, white aprons, white caps, and low heeled shoes. They were all well trained to serve at parties like this. They were all smiling. It went off without a hitch, unless something happened out of sight.

The party was at 2 p.m. so the food needed to be light. The kitchen staff went above and beyond. Joanne was in her element. It was like she was in a zone. The food was prepared and put on the platters like an assembly line. Finger sandwiches and petite desserts were served by the staff with tongs from a silver platter.

MENU

Ham and Mustard on White
Cucumber Mint and Cream Cheese
Egg with Watercress
Chicken Salad on Toast
Roast Beef and Cucumber on Rye

Strawberry Shortcake Trifle
Chocolate Coffee Mousse
Mini Pecan Pie
Mini Lemon Meringue Tort
Mini Cherry Cheesecake

Everything was served on delicate Bavarian china sandwich plates. The teacups were also Bavarian china. No two place settings were alike though. Miss Peg wanted the variety. It all went off without a problem. Once everyone had been served, Miss Peg stood up to speak. This speech was to dispel any rumors that might be floating around. She explained the entire story. Patrick was to blame right along with James. James would pay the price though for not doing what was right in the first place.

There were some questions like "Will he really serve any hard time?" Things of that nature. She answered all of them to the best of her knowledge. Everyone seemed content with the answers.

It all wound down around 5 p.m. It appeared the ladies were happy that they came. It was always nice to get together with friends to catch up. The one person Miss Peg wished had been there wasn't; Laura Parker. The Prosecutor felt it was best if they weren't seen together. It was hard on both of them but they complied.

Once this mess with James was over and done with, Miss Peg hoped Laura would consider coming back to work for her. The mood at the house was much different back then when she was there. The staff remained respectful, but, there wasn't as much joy and laughter as when Laura managed the house. She missed that.

Chapter 27

September 11 saw a media circus around the courthouse. This small town wasn't used to this much publicity. The Prosecutor didn't expect the trial to garner this much interest. The trial was supposed to start at 9 a.m., but there were people standing in line at 6 a.m., to be in the gallery. Kester Municipal Police were directing all the traffic and media trucks. They were caught off guard. Tomorrow and the time for the rest of the trial would be different. There were a lot of police officers getting paid overtime.

James entered the courtroom at about ten minutes to nine and joined his attorney at the defense table. His attorney wanted him there earlier than that but the traffic around the courthouse was so congested the transport officers couldn't get there any earlier.

He was dressed in one of his expensive suits and ties. His hair had been neatly trimmed. His suit looked too large for him. The jail food wasn't what James was used to so he hadn't been eating. It's hard to say how much weight he had lost. He looked drawn. Being in jail for over three months did him no favors. It was only going to get worse before it got better.

Miss Peg was in the gallery but not where James expected her to be sitting. She was sitting in the second row behind the Prosecutor's table. When James saw this the frown and look of anger on his face was apparent that he was not pleased.

Laura, Elizabeth, and Jeremiah sat in the first row right behind the Prosecutor. The Prosecutor was talking in low tones to Laura. None of the Parker children especially wanted to be there but felt they should be. They just wanted this nightmare to end once and for all.

Bailiff: "All rise. The Honorable Brandon Matthews presiding. (Pause.) Be seated."

Judge Matthews entered the courtroom at 9 a.m. sharp. There was a lot of chatter in the gallery. The Judge had to bang his gavel quite a few times to quiet the courtroom. You could tell by the look on his face that he wasn't pleased.

Judge: "Mr. Jacobs, are you ready to proceed with jury selection?"

Lenny Jacobs: "The people are ready, Your Honor."

Judge: "Mr. Bishop, are you ready to proceed with jury selection?"

Bishop: "We renew our request that all charges against Mr. Martin be dropped due to insufficient evidence."

Judge: "Mr. Bishop, this will be the third time I've said this. This trial will proceed. Are you ready for jury selection or not?"

Bishop: "Unhappily, yes, Your Honor."

Judge: "Fine. Bailiff, will you please set the first panel of potential jurors?"

The Bailiff brought in the first twelve people to sit down in the jury box. The attorneys questioned each one of them, allowing some and dismissing some. The back and forth went on all morning. In all, the attorneys questioned thirty people. By noon though they had impaneled a jury with one alternate.

Judge: "Instead of returning this afternoon, as I have other obligations, we will reconvene at 9 a.m. tomorrow. Court adjourned."

The chatter in the gallery started up immediately. Miss Peg and the Parkers needed police assistance to get out of the courtroom, and the courthouse. They had to huddle together to get out safely. This was only the beginning of all the questioning and shouting they would have to endure from the media.

Chapter 28

The trial lasted for five days not counting jury deliberation. Miss Peg, Laura, and Benjamin were all called to testify as to what James had confessed to them. Sheriff Stone and Deputy Richard Friend testified about the car and its location. Deputy Friend also testified to the old odor of alcohol in the car when he opened the door.

Mr. Bishop objected to their testimonies as all hearsay and should be excluded. He argued that finding the car had nothing to do with his client.

Judge: "Mr. Bishop, this has all been relevant as far as I'm concerned. Save this all for your closing argument. Due to the late hour, we will adjourn until 9 a.m. tomorrow. The jury is instructed to not discuss today's testimony with anyone. Court is dismissed.

This was only day four. James never took the stand.

Day five dawned with the Prosecutor giving his closing argument. He put the four days of testimony together into one compact package. He explained to the jury how James had hidden the fact that the car that had killed David Parker had been concealed. The accident happened almost eight years ago, and James had known about it for about seven of those years. He told how James had profited by not saying anything – not even to his mother.

Jacobs: "It's really sad, Ladies and Gentlemen of the Jury, that the desire for money was more important than bringing justice to David Parker and his family. James Martin was angry because his father died way too soon. He was angry because his father drank so much that he was rarely there for the family. The fact that his father died from drinking to excess made him angry. Instead of being angry with his father though for all of this, he blamed David Parker, for being where he was, on his bike, coming home from work. As an extension he blamed Laura Parker. They didn't just not get along, he was angry with her because of the guilt his father felt for killing her father. "This case is about *misplaced anger*, ladies and gentlemen. He was angry at the wrong person and allowed that anger to grow until it boiled over that Sunday afternoon. Please don't kid yourself. He was very drunk but all the alcohol did was loosen his tongue. Instead of feeling bad for all his years of deceit he was angry and decided to take it out on Laura Parker—the one innocent person in all of this."

"Put yourself in the shoes of the children. First they lose their father to a hit-and-run driver. Then, probably out of grief, three years later they lose their mother. The oldest had to become a parent at twenty-one for two teenage siblings. Their lives had changed drastically. Barely a year after their father's death, James Martin discovered the car that killed David Parker. When he questioned his father he found out the truth. He chose to keep this to himself. In exchange he received money, cars, and expensive trips. All the time, the three children were mourning their parents. That, ladies and gentlemen, should not stand. Thank you. I rest my case."

Edward Bishop stood up and walked to the jury box.

Bishop: "Good morning, Ladies and Gentlemen. First I want to thank you all for your attention during the trial. I've watched you all and know that you all know what the right decision should be. Mr. Jacob wants you to make a decision to send a man to jail for things people believe he said and knew. Mr. Martin was a son that loved his father and felt he needed to protect him from unfounded accusations."

"On a Sunday afternoon, after a Saturday night of heavy drinking, he came home to find his mother talking with her house manager, Laura Parker. Mr. Martin and Miss Parker had not liked each other very much since they were teenagers. Several years ago she slapped him the day after her mother died because he teased her about something that had nothing to do with her mother's death. The Prosecutor failed to inform you of her violent nature. She used this incident, on this Sunday, to get back at him for his teasing."

"His mother 'sent him to his room' after his so-called confession telling him to shower and sober up. During her testimony, Mr. Martin's mother admitted that he was prone to exaggeration all his life. She could not, in all good conscience, know if his story that day was exaggerated or not. Sheriff Stone asked the witnesses to the accident that killed David Parker if the car he had towed from the Martins' was definitely the one in the accident. None of them could positively identify Mr. Martin's Mercedes as the one that hit and killed Mr. Parker. So, the car they found could not be identified as the evidence my client supposedly kept from law enforcement. The Prosecutor had no way of proving that my client knew for a fact that his father was actually the driver. All the testimony here has been hearsay from a heavily intoxicated person."

"When Mr. Martin's father passed away, his mother stopped giving Mr. Martin the money his father felt he deserved. Was Mr. Martin angry? Yes. In his state of intoxication though could he have relayed such a detailed account of an accident from almost eight years ago? No. He told a story to make Miss Parker leave the family home as a staff member once and for all. She no longer worked for Mrs. Martin as of that Sunday, so, he obtained his objective. But, the story he told them that day was all fiction. They took it for the truth and ran with it to the Sheriff."

"Hearsay and unfounded truths should not be held against Mr. Martin to send him to jail. Bottom line, should Mr. Martin go to jail because he and Miss Parker didn't get along? Your answer should be no. I believe you can all see through the fiction in these stories and find my client not guilty of all charges. Thank you again for your attention."

With that Mr. Bishop sat down.

The chatter in the courtroom was silenced with one hit of the Judge's gavel.

Judge: "Ladies and Gentlemen, it is lunchtime. I know you plan on working this afternoon on this case. I will close out this section of proceedings and let you have your lunch. We will convene at 1:30 p.m. I will give you your instructions then. Enjoy whatever lunch you ordered. Court is adjourned until 1:30 p.m. today."

The jury filed out of the courtroom after the Judge left. The Bailiff escorted James back to his cell. The gallery was then allowed to leave. James's attorney requested a meeting over lunch with Mr. Jacob.

Bishop: "I think you've lost the jury. No way are they going to convict my client. To save some time though we would entertain a plea agreement... reasonable of course."

Jacobs: "I'm not even going to make an offer. I'll let the jury make that decision. As you told them, they were paying attention. My witnesses told it all. There was no one defending James' actions. They'll go with the one that gave them the most information. See you back in court."

At 1:30 p.m. the jury returned along with the Judge. It looked like people had changed seats in the gallery to make it possible for other people to come in.

Judge Matthews pounded his gavel.

Judge: "Let's have some quiet in here. If not I'll just clear the courtroom. (Silence.) Now, Ladies and Gentlemen of the Jury, it is your turn to take over this case. You have been given all the information from both sides of this case. It is your job to weigh all the evidence and decide who was telling the truth. Your decision must be made beyond a shadow of a doubt. You are to leave emotions out of your decision as much as possible. It is the law that is to be decided.

"You will not be sequestered but will stay as late as you deem necessary. If you do not reach a verdict today you will be sent home under a gag order and resume deliberations at 9 a.m. tomorrow. You are now dismissed to start your deliberations. Court will stand in recess until the jury can return with a verdict. Court adjourned."

It was 2:00 p.m. The courtroom quickly cleared out and the crowd congregated on the steps. As in the past, as Miss Peg, Laura, Elizabeth, and Jeremiah left, they were surrounded by reporters firing off question after question. The police were still guarding them to get them safely to their cars. They were torn as to what to do. Should they stay around and hope for a quick decision, or go home and wait for what might be a late call? They weren't that far from the courthouse, so they went home. That was the only place they felt safe right now anyway.

Chapter 29

As with the last five days, Miss Peg and the Parkers were escorted by the police. Both driveways were blocked off to prevent any vehicles, except those of police and property owners, from entering. For some reason this case had received a lot of attention across the state. There was a large media presence all over town.

The fact that the Martin family owned a manufacturing company with international ties had the most to due with it. Patrick was known to have commercial dealings around the world. The national level was even more apparent. The Board of Directors were concerned that this trial and all the accusations could affect their bottom line. So far nothing negative had been seen, but, nonetheless, the Board members were nervous.

Everyone tried to go about their normal activities but they were all distracted by what could be going on in the jury room. To them the answer was cut and dry. It would have been an emotional answer for them. The Prosecutor laid it all out the way it had happened.

Everyone who testified told the truth. It had to go their way. The attorney for James just wanted the jury to feel sorry for James. None of this was his fault...boohoo. He just wanted it all without paying the price. The Parkers paid the price.

6:30 p.m. The phone rang. Laura jumped to answer it.

Jacobs: "The jury chose to stay past the 5 p.m. hour as usual, because they were close to a verdict. Good thing they did. The verdict is in. We're to be in court at 7 p.m. to hear it. You should be there. Mrs. Martin has also been notified."

Laura: "Oh we'll be there; you can count on that. I'll let security know we'll be leaving. Thank you for calling, Mr. Jacobs."

Jacobs: "You're welcome...I'll see you shortly."

Chapter 30

Word had quickly gotten out that the jury had a verdict. Every available seat in the gallery was filled. Interested citizens and the media were either standing in the back of the courtroom, in the hallway, or on the courthouse steps. Everyone seemed to be talking at once. The reporters pounced on Miss Peg and the Parker children as they came up the courthouse steps. Their police security was having to fight to keep them safe as they entered the courthouse. It was the same inside as they maneuvered their way into the courtroom.

It was 6:55 p.m.

At 7 p.m., the Judge entered the courtroom. As he sat down he had to again pound his gavel several times to quiet the spectators in the courtroom.

Judge: "I want silence. If you all don't settle down I will have the Bailiffs clear the courtroom of anyone not directly involved in this case. Do I make myself clear?"

The courtroom became very quiet.

Judge: "Bailiffs, will you please position yourselves around the room so you can remove anyone that becomes disruptive?"

The Bailiffs moved around to the four corners and down the aisle of the gallery.

Judge: "Regardless of what decision the jury comes back with I expect silence. Anyone that becomes unruly will be immediately removed. This has been a trial full of emotions. I won't have any outbursts. If that is clear, Bailiff, will you bring in the defendant?"

James came in wearing cuffs. The Bailiff removed them and James sat down with his attorney.

Judge: "Now, Bailiff, will you please bring in the jury?"

The Bailiff opened the door to the jury room. The room was hushed. All you heard was the shuffling of the feet of the jury as they moved to their seats. All the jurors were looking down at the floor, no eye contact with either side of the aisle. Once they were seated the Judge turned to them:

Judge: "Mr. Foreman, I understand you have reached a verdict."

Foreman: "We have, Your Honor."

Judge: "Will you please hand it to the Clerk?"

The Clerk took the sheet of paper with the verdict from the Foreman and handed it to the Judge. Without any expression on his face the Judge read the verdict and handed it back to the Clerk, who then handed it back to the Foreman.

Judge: "Will the defendant please rise?"

James and his attorney stood up, buttoned their jackets and stared at the jurors.

Judge: "Mr. Foreman, will you please read your verdict as to Count 1, Obstruction of Justice?"

Foreman: "We, the jury, find James Martin; guilty."

The courtroom erupted behind the defendant's table. The Judge pounded his gavel several times.

Judge: "One more outburst and you'll not only be ejected but also arrested. AM I CLEAR?"

"Mr. Foreman, will you please read your verdict as to Count 2, Accessory After the Fact of Second Degree Vehicular Manslaughter?"

Foreman: "We, the jury, find James Martin guilty."

The reporters in the courtroom rushed out to make phone calls to their respective media with the verdict. GUILTY ON BOTH COUNTS.

The Parker children pulled each other together and simply hugged each other. Tears flowed down their faces. There was finally justice for their father. Laura couldn't help but think, *Too bad Mom wasn't here to see this.*

Judge: "Ladies and Gentlemen of the Jury, thank you for your attention to this matter. We will convene on Tuesday, September 18 at 9 a.m. to begin the sentencing phase. Mr. Martin will be remanded into custody. Court adjourned."

James' friends were shouting encouraging words to him and obscenities to Laura. The Bailiffs were doing their best to clear the courtroom so the Parkers and Miss Peg could leave safely.

Chapter 31

The next week was not pleasant for Miss Peg or the Parkers. Both of their phone numbers had gotten out so their phones rang nonstop. Laura shut off her cell phone and took the house phone off the hook. Miss Peg unhooked all her phones. Neither of them could believe the ugly phone calls they were getting. It shocked them that so many people felt James should not have been found guilty. There were probably some positive calls but they weren't received because they stopped answering their phone entirely.

The mail started, too. You would think James was a celebrity the way people were treating his conviction. The problem was he wouldn't be around to shower his friends with the free money he had been receiving. All his so-called friends would have to fund their own parties, and nights of drinking. It was unfortunate that money becomes such a significant factor in relationships.

Laura heard that Trinity was devastated by the verdict. The life she had hoped for with James would now not come to pass. She envisioned living in the

Martin Estate, and not having to work a day in her life. She'd have a staff do everything for her like they now did for Miss Peg. She would have all the money she wanted for clothes and entertaining. As it turned out now though she'd have to put her degree in journalism to work. Maybe her dad would give her a job at the *News-Sentinel*. Her first story could be the one where James finally got caught ignoring the truth.

Chapter 32

By September 18, the media circus hadn't slowed down. They had dubbed James Martin as "Kester's Golden Child." The media have been talking to James' friends.

According to the friends they talked to, James was a saint. He was generous with his time and money. They said he didn't have any enemies. The one thing all his friends agreed on was that he and Laura Parker did not get along. No one knew why. Most of them didn't know Laura. They had seen her around at the Martin Estate but for the most part that was it. Some of them remembered seeing her on the college campus years ago.

One of the reporters talked to Trinity, who was still a mess emotionally, about James being convicted. She told the reporter they had planned to get married. He was supposed to take over his family's manufacturing factory. Since his father died, he had been working with management to learn everything to step into his father's shoes. Now she doubted any of that would happen. She definitely didn't know that Miss Peg had no intention of turning the company over to him. He obviously was stringing Trinity along.

The courtroom was again packed. Miss Peg and the Parkers were there early. Their security stood close because some people outside the courthouse were yelling threats and angry comments at them. The people that were on their side were yelling at the angry protesters. The shouting match had become unreal.

At 8:55 a.m., the Bailiff brought James into the courtroom. He had enough time to talk to some of his friends and scowl at his mother and Laura. He still felt he was not guilty of doing anything wrong. All he did was not say anything to anyone. The jury felt differently. Today they would put a sentence to the crime. Right after James sat down the jury was seated.

Judge Matthews walked in at 9 a.m., sharp, as usual. He sat down and then silenced the courtroom with his gavel. He had his "no nonsense" look on his face.

Judge: "The first order of business will be jury instructions. After that will be the Victim Impact Statements. When that is completed, the jury will retire to make their sentencing recommendation."

"Jail time for Obstruction of Justice is five to ten years, with a $25,000 fine. For Accessory After the Fact of Second Degree Vehicular Manslaughter is three to five years with again a $25,000 fine. Ladies and Gentlemen of the Jury, these are the years you have to work with. No matter what part you do, these times will run consecutively. In other words, one right after another. Because of that, you can take these years and use them as you feel fit the crime. "For example, you can take the five years for obstruction and just the three years for accessory, so he would serve eight years. Or, if you feel he should serve the maximum, you can make it ten years for obstruction and five years for accessory. You don't need to use these numbers at all. This is just an example. You can mix them up however you see fit. You have all the years to work with. You'll be able to come up with something fair. The $25,000 fine for each however stands. Are there any questions? Okay, no questions. We will listen to the Victim Impact Statement then you can deliberate on sentencing."

"Miss Laura Parker, would you please step up to the podium and read us your statement?"

Laura got up and walked to the podium. There was a lot of chatter and booing. Again the Judge had to bang his gavel several times to quiet the room.

Judge: "Bailiff, if there are any more disruptions you have my permission to remove that person and place them under arrest. I have made it clear in the past. I will not put up with any more disruptions. Am I clear? I am sorry, Miss Parker. Please continue with your statement."

Laura: "Thank you, Your Honor. Eight years ago, Patrick Martin hit my father, and killed him, then drove away. Law enforcement searched high and low, but the car was never found. A year after the accident, James Martin found his father's damaged silver Mercedes in the boat shed on their property. When asked about it, Patrick told the truth about it. He explained his actions completely to James. He needed to unburden himself to someone. He thought James would keep his secret. He did, but, there was a price attached: new cars, expensive parties, trips, and all the money he could spend."

"Now, Patrick had been a heavy drinker for years. In the years right before he died though it got worse. That is what eventually killed him."

"I went to Central Illinois University for a year. I had seen James Martin but never spoke to him. I just wasn't in his circle of friends. I dropped out of college when my dad was killed and went to work for Miss Peg—uh, Mrs. Martin, to help support our family. Somewhere along the line, James remembered seeing me on campus. It was around this time he came up with a name for me...Dogpatch. (There was laughing in the gallery—a pounding of the Judge's gavel.) I've never understood the name but just ignored it. That was also when he just started teasing and harassing me. Don't ask me why, because I don't have the answer to that."

"It wasn't long after I started to work for the Martins that James seemed to come into a lot of money, and more freedom. He had a couple of years of college to finish, but was partying a lot more. I just attributed it to his getting older."

"About a year after he graduated from college Patrick Martin died. James became a very angry person. His father's death must have hit him pretty hard. I came into Miss Peg's office, right after Patrick died, as James came storming out. My concern was for Miss Peg. She said he just didn't get his way."

"The years after Patrick died made James just a not so nice person. His drinking increased, and he was downright mean to all the staff. He was especially nasty to me."

"My mother died a year after Patrick. I went to the Martins' to inform Miss Peg, since my mother worked for her. It was this morning when I had been accused by Mr. Bishop of having a violent nature. I put up with name-calling from James but did not put up with his using derogatory names about my brother and sister. He came in, called me Dogpatch, then made the nasty comment: 'I see you have the two Mud Puddles with you.' I snapped. I am not a violent person, but I would no longer tolerate his disrespect...especially on the day my mother died."

"Over the years after my parents died, I have been the guardian of my brother and sister and the adult in the house. My parents were determined we all would go to college and pursue our dreams. That takes money. Both of my parents worked extra jobs to make sure the college money was there. It's been a struggle, because I now work three jobs to make sure the college money is there. Elizabeth and Jeremiah graduated this year, with honors. They've worked extra hard to already be ahead, for two years, in their college studies. The money I earn will go to their post-graduate studies as well. They have done all of this while their emotions are raw from the loss of both their parents."

"The one downside—and don't get me wrong, I'm not complaining—is that I have never had the time to have a social life of my own. Being mom and dad and the only breadwinner doesn't leave much time for anything for yourself. Under the circumstances, I wouldn't have had it any other way. They come first."

"The point of all of this is this: If Patrick or James had owned up to killing my father, things would probably be a lot different. My mother missed my father, terribly, but the difficult part for her was she didn't know who did it or why. I do believe she would still be alive today if only James had spoken up and done the right thing."

"I apologize, Your Honor, for this lengthy diatribe, but I needed to get it out. The jury should know how the inaction of James made our family hurt the way we do. We're strong but should not have had to gain our strength the way we did. Thank you all for listening to what I had to say."

With that Laura sat down and grabbed Elizabeth's and Jeremiah's hands. The courtroom was silent. Even the hecklers were quiet. The Judge just sat there like everyone else.

Judge: "Thank you, Miss Parker, for your statement. Is there anyone else, impacted by this case, who would like to speak?"

With that, James jumped up.

James: "I should be able to make a statement to counteract what she just said."

Judge: "Sit down, Mr. Martin. You had ample time to testify during the trial, and you chose not to. You are not a victim in any of this. SIT DOWN! Mr. Bishop, control your client."

Bishop: "My apologies, Your Honor."

James sat down but continued to grumble.

Judge: "Unless there is anyone else that wants to speak I'll turn this over to the jury."

He pauses.

Judge: "Okay, Ladies and Gentlemen, I will release you now to determine what the sentence should be for James Martin. I have explained your choices. Take your time and let the Clerk know when you are ready to let the rest of us know. With that, court is dismissed for now."

The Judge pounded the gavel and left the courtroom. It got very noisy in there. The Prosecutor told Miss Peg and the Parkers that this phase of the trial usually doesn't take very long.

Jacobs: "Once they convict the defendant, they're ready to be done with this. I doubt it'll take more than a couple of hours. If you want you can just go down to the cafeteria for a cup of coffee to wait. That's where I'm headed. Your security will keep anyone away. After your statement though I doubt anyone, even the hecklers, will bother you. Follow me. Officers, come with us. About now, I can really use a cup of coffee."

Less than two hours later, the Clerk called Mr. Jacobs and told him the jury was back.

Jacobs: "See? What did I tell you? They're ready to wash their hands of this and go home."

Once everyone was back in the courtroom, and the Judge was seated, the Bailiff brought in the jury.

Judge: "Ladies and Gentlemen of the Jury, I understand you have decided on a sentence for Mr. Martin. Will you please hand the Clerk your decision?"

Once he had the decision, he read it and handed it back to the Clerk—without any expression.

Judge: "Mr. Foreman, will you please read your decision?"

Foreman: "Yes, Your Honor. The unanimous decision of all the jurors is that Mr. Martin should serve the maximum of both sentences. The total years before he will be eligible for parole is fifteen years. The jurors also want to tell the Parker children that they are very sorry for their loss and all they have been put through."

The gallery again erupted with angry shouts. The Bailiffs wasted no time this time clearing the courtroom of the unruly spectators.

Judge: "Anyone want to go to jail? One more sound, and that's where you'll be headed. (All quiet.) Ladies and Gentlemen, I thank you for your consideration in this matter. I know it was a difficult decision to make. With that, the jury is excused. Mr. Martin, you will be taken back to your cell while the Department of Corrections decides which facility you will go to. It's time to pay for your deeds. This case is closed...court dismissed."

The Parker family just sat there stunned. James would pay dearly for his deception. Miss Peg stood up and put her hands on Laura's shoulders. When Laura turned around, Miss Peg had one short thing to say.

Miss Peg: "It's over, child. Time to move on."

Chapter 33

They did move on. It was easier now. They knew who was to blame for their dad's death. In Church, they were taught to forgive. At this point though they hadn't gotten there yet. They couldn't understand how they were supposed to do that. What was supposed to be a joyous time for all of them now that college was behind them still had a cloud over it.

It had been over two years since the trial. They had all been busy with their own lives. Laura didn't seem to be able to back away from her jobs. She seemed to like cleaning for other people. She did go back and work for Miss Peg a couple of days a week. It just wasn't the same since James' revelation. There were Christmas parties and garden parties Miss Peg always needed help with. Laura just chuckled every time she asked for help. Miss Peg had been organizing parties long before Laura was around. She just seemed to want Laura around as much as possible. Miss Peg never got tired of eating Laura's freshly baked bread, so she requested it often. When Laura started at the Martins' over ten years earlier her job was baking the bread for the family. Miss Peg still requested it. She even had

Laura bake the sandwich bread for the parties. She more than obliged.

Laura was simply enjoying her life right now. The reason she was only working a couple of days a week was that she decided to go back to college. She was only taking one class right now though. Now that the twins were well on their way she'd work on her future. She knew that at one class a semester it would take a lot of years to finish college with just a Bachelor's Degree but she was enjoying herself just the same. Her parents would be very pleased that she was at least trying.

Elizabeth and Jeremiah had grown into mature young adults, far from the gangly eleven-year-olds when they lost their father.

Elizabeth was tall and thin like her mother. Like Laura she wore her blond hair long.

Jeremiah had grown to be built like a football player, broad shoulders and solid muscles.

Elizabeth had secured a job with one of the best cardiologists in the area. He found out she was on her way to being a PA, so he took her under his wing. On the days she wasn't studying medicine in school, she practiced it with the doctor. She was in seventh heaven. She was well on her way to her dream. Her mom and dad would be incredibly proud of her. All their hard work and now Laura's was paying off.

The other exciting thing for Elizabeth was that in a little under a year, she would be marrying her high school sweetheart. In January of the following year, she'd marry Carl Nance, the young man who had escorted her to her senior prom. He had one more year of college before becoming a pharmacist. They were a cute couple and complemented each other. Life for them was just starting and looking up.

Jeremiah was doing just as well. His culinary skills were exceptional. So much so that he had earned a six month fellowship to study in France. It took much longer than that to become a French chef, but he would learn the rudimentary skills needed to master some of the amazing French dishes. He'd learn chocolate and pastry skills as well. One step closer to gaining his dream.

He was also getting married. In March of the following year he would also marry his high school sweetheart, Georgette Summers, the girl he had escorted to his senior prom. She had a couple more years for her Master's Degree in Mathematics. She planned on teaching when she got out of school.

Both Parker children had worked hard to achieve the goals they set for themselves many years earlier. The death of their parents seemed to only further fuel their ambitions. They had chosen well in careers and life partners. Nothing would stop them now.

Chapter 34

Laura pulled into her driveway on a beautiful May day. She was greeted by the beautiful flowers along the front of her house. Her mom and Aunt Connie had planted azaleas and rhododendron bushes about fifteen years earlier. They were huge, and in full bloom as were the irises and tulips. It was quite the floral showpiece.

As she got out of the car she waved to her neighbor, Beatrice Walker. Beatrice was a little woman, short with a slight build. Her curly gray hair just bounced when she laughed. She was out walking her two dogs—Brutus, a full- grown rottweiler, and Zeus, a king shepherd. These were two very well-trained dogs. Beatrice was retired and lived alone so had the dogs for protection. Their area had never had any crime but she felt better having the dogs. She had them trained professionally to respond to commands only she knew and that they'd respond to from her. The dogs loved Laura, so Beatrice taught them to respond to her, too. You never know. She had the dogs on a leash, which was unusual until Laura saw why—a FedEx truck just went down the road. For some reason, the dogs did not like those trucks. Beatrice would let them run loose when the truck left.

Laura set down her purse and the bag of groceries and took out her phone. She decided to make a video and send it to her Aunt Connie so she could see how beautiful the flowers all looked. As she was recording, she talked to Aunt Connie.

Laura: "Look how beautiful all the flowers look today, Aunt Connie. I know Mom is looking down and smiling. I wish you were here to see them in person, but I guess this will have to be the next best thing. The rhododendron…"

There was a loud roar of a truck pulling into the driveway. Laura turned abruptly. It was the large black pickup owned by Matt Roman. Along with him were Derek Sanders, and Andrew Cassidy, good friends of James Martin. All three of them jumped out of the truck. Matt left the truck running.

Laura: (Angrily) "What are you guys doing here? I didn't think I'd ever have to see you again."

Matt rushed up to her—

Matt: "Hey, Dogpatch, Jim Martin says 'hello.'"

At this he swung full force with his right balled-up fist and hit Laura in the jaw. The force was so strong you could hear her bones break. The force knocked her out, and she fell to the ground unconscious. She was lying on her right side. One of the men went around to the front of her and kicked her in the abdomen. It turned out to be Derek Sanders.

Matt: "We'll show you what happens when you mess with the wrong people."

Derek: "You didn't think we would forget how you took everything away from us did you?"

Andrew: "We had it made until you showed up. You won't get away with what you've done."

Derek: "We'll make sure you never have the chance to do anything to anyone else."

Beatrice saw this happen and yelled.

Beatrice: "What are you men doing? Leave her alone."

With that, she dropped the dogs' leashes and yelled:

Beatrice: "IGEN!"

Both dogs took off running, barking, and growling. The three men saw the two dogs and yelled.

Derek: "Shit! Let's go. I don't want to mess with those dogs."

All three bolted for the truck but not quickly enough. Zeus caught Derek by the arm and wasn't letting go.

Derek: "GET HIM OFF ME. GET HIM OFF!"

Beatrice: "NEM!"

Zeus let loose but not before he had torn Derek's arm up pretty good. Matt put the truck in reverse and spun his way out of the yard. The passenger door was still open as Derek was struggling to get in. Beatrice ran to Laura. Brutus was lying next to her whining. Zeus joined him. Beatrice grabbed her cell phone out of her pocket and dialed 911.

911 Operator: "911, what is the address of your emergency?"

Beatrice: "Uh, 52493 Sweet Spring Road. I need the police and an ambulance. Three Men just attacked my neighbor lady. She's unconscious and I think her jaw is broken. Please hurry!"

911 Operator: "Ma'am, is she breathing?"

Beatrice: "Yes, but it is very shallow. Besides hitting her one of them gave her a very hard kick in the stomach. Please hurry!! Oh, God, she can't die!!"

911 Operator: "Just stay with her. Help is on the way. Do I hear some whining in the background?"

Beatrice: "Yes, it's my dogs. I think they may have saved her life. They scared off the attackers. As a matter of fact, one of my dogs actually got hold of one of their arms."

911 Operator: "Ma'am, your dogs sound very protective. Maybe you should confine them before help gets there. They may not let the EMTs get close to the victim."

Beatrice: "You're right. I just don't want to leave Laura by herself. I'll...I'll just run and put them in the yard. JÖN."

Beatrice quickly walked the dogs to her fenced-in yard. She wasn't able to run. As she headed back to Laura she could hear the sirens.

Chapter 35

Before the ambulance got there, Beatrice picked up Laura's phone. She needed to call Elizabeth. She noticed the camera app was open, but she really didn't give that a second thought. Once she found Elizabeth's name in the contacts she called her.

Beatrice: "Elizabeth, it isn't Laura. It's Beatrice from across the road. Three men just came by and attacked Laura. The police and an ambulance are just pulling up. I don't know how far away you are, but maybe you should just head to the ER."

Elizabeth: (Very excitedly) "Do you know how badly Laura is hurt? Please tell me more. I'll call Jeremiah. I hear the siren. Do you have any idea who they were? Have you seen them around there before?"

Beatrice: "She is unconscious right now so I can't ask her how she feels. I saw one hit her in the face but I can't tell you much more than that. I have no idea who they were. One will be hurting pretty bad though because Zeus got hold of him."

Elizabeth: "Good dog."

Beatrice: "I'm not sure what to do about Laura's phone. When I picked it up to call you the camera app was open. She may have gotten a picture of who did this."

Elizabeth: "I'm five minutes away. Hold on to it. It'll take the EMTs a few minutes to get her ready to transport. I'll get the phone from you."

Beatrice: "Oh good, Sheriff Stone is here. He must have been close. I'll see you in a few minutes."

"Hello, Sheriff Stone, I'm Beatrice Walker, Laura's neighbor. This is terrible. Laura was just out here looking at her flowers when this black truck pulled up and three men got out. OH MY! She is really hurt!"

Zeus and Brutus can be heard howling in the background. The sirens hurt their ears. There are strange people around Beatrice and Laura, too. That didn't make them happy.

Sheriff: "Ms. Walker, can you describe the truck or the men? Have you ever seen them before?"

Beatrice: "It was a big black shiny pickup. I can't tell you what kind though. I think I saw the men in the courtroom at James Martin's trial. The blond one is the one that kicked Laura in the stomach. I didn't see who hit her though. The truck was in the way."

Sheriff: (Angrily) "Derek Sanders!"

Beatrice: "The blond one will need medical care for his arm. My dog, Zeus, got hold of him and really dug in."

Sheriff: "That fact will be very helpful. Thank you, Ms. Walker. These poor kids. They've really had it rough—now this."

Just then, Elizabeth pulled up. The EMTs were still working to stabilize Laura before they could transport her to the hospital. It took a couple of rolls of gauze to wrap around her head to immobilize her jaw, before they could put a collar on her. The Sheriff had to hold Elizabeth back so they could work. They noticed her right arm was also broken from when she fell. They felt her abdomen and were concerned that there may be some severe injury there as well.

Beatrice went to Elizabeth and pulled her into her arms. At the same time, she gave her Laura's phone.

Beatrice: "You might want to check the camera app and see if she got any pictures of who had done this."

Elizabeth took the phone and turned on the app. The look on her face was one of horror. She took the phone over to Sheriff Stone.

Elizabeth: "Sheriff, you're going to want to see this. Laura was taking a video of the front of the house to send to our Aunt Connie when these guys pulled up. They definitely surprised her, because she turned around very quickly. She didn't get a video of the entire attack, only the beginning, but the audio was still on. These are the cowards that attacked my sister."

The Sheriff just shook his head. He had suspicions that it was these three men, but now he had proof. Laura had inadvertently recorded her whole attack. They wouldn't be able to deny this.

Sheriff: "Send that video to my phone. I'm going to take that to the Prosecutor to get an arrest warrant for these three. James Martin hasn't given up tormenting

Laura, has he? If at all possible, he'll be charged with this, too."

It took about twenty minutes for the EMTs to have Laura ready to take her to the hospital. Moving her was difficult considering her injuries. Once they had her on the stretcher though they were out of the yard in minutes.

Elizabeth's phone rang. It was Jeremiah. She had called him but could only leave him a message. He was in class in Chicago when she called him. He still had an almost five-hour drive to get home. She explained it all to him and begged him to drive carefully. She knew he was upset but didn't want anything to happen to him. She promised she would let him know if her condition changed. Right now she was stable.

Chapter 36

It was about two hours after Laura was taken to the hospital that Elizabeth found out how badly she had been hurt. The Sheriff spent most of that time with her. He needed to know what he would charge the three men responsible with. Considering what Matt Roman said before he hit Laura, he would also charge James Martin. It looked like he was the one behind the attack.

Dr. Reynolds, ER doctor: "Miss Parker? Your sister is on her way to surgery. We will have to wait to do any repairs on her jaw. That is very bad but we have her on a vent so she's stable that way. The X-rays though show that her abdomen is filling with blood. We have blood running now but we need to go in and see where the blood is coming from so we can stop it. There is a lot of blood in her urine so I'm hoping that isn't where all the blood is coming from. We can tell by the scan that we'll have to remove her spleen at least but beyond that I don't know how bad it is. I need to go...I'll let you know what we had to do when I'm done. It'll be a couple of hours before I have any answers."

Elizabeth: "Will she survive this?"

Dr. Reynolds: "We'll do our best to make sure she does."

With that the doctor quickly left. Elizabeth just sat down and finally let the tears go. The Sheriff sat there with her until she was able to pull herself together.

Sheriff: "Is there anyone I can call for you so you aren't alone?"

Elizabeth: "No, thank you, Sheriff. My brother is on his way from Chicago. He'll be here in a couple of hours. I called him from the house and he was on his way home then. I worry about him having to drive knowing about this but I'll just have to pray he makes it here safely."

Sheriff: "I'm going to go see the Prosecutor right now. I will see if he'll issue the arrest warrants yet tonight. Those three don't deserve to be sitting and celebrating what they have done any longer. The hospital and all the medical centers have been alerted to let me know if Derek comes in to have his arm treated from the attack by Ms. Walker's dog. I want to see him explain that away. Are you sure I can't call someone?"

Elizabeth: "No, really. I'll be fine. I want to call Miss Peg and let her know what has happened. Since Laura will be in surgery for a couple of hours, maybe I'll just run out there and tell her. Telling her will ease my mind anyway. Jim is involved so she needs to know. Thank you, Sheriff. You've been a great help. I'll keep you informed, too, on how she's doing."

With that they both left the ER waiting room. Elizabeth called Jeremiah and gave him the update on Laura's condition. She was still worried about him driving under this cloud but he promised he was driving the speed limit and was being careful. She told him what she was going to do and that she would be back at the hospital before he got there. Then...out of a habit they had all developed...she told him she loved him before she hung up.

Chapter 37

Usually, the drive to see Miss Peg was a joyful one. Not tonight. It was a little after 9 p.m. The sun had set so twilight made the purpose even more mournful.

When Miss Peg answered the door and saw Elizabeth standing there, her heart sank.

Miss Peg: "The last time a Parker girl stood at my door this late at night, she told me someone had died. Please don't say that is why you're here. Has something happened to Laura or Jeremiah?"

Elizabeth was already close to tears when she told her.

Elizabeth: "Three men attacked Laura at home tonight. She was outside when they pulled up. One hit her in the jaw, broke it and knocked her out. One of the others kicked her in the stomach while she was on the ground. If the neighbor's dogs hadn't attacked, they probably would have killed her. You need to know. It looks like Jim may have sent them over there to do it. Laura was taking a video of the front of the house when they attacked her. Her camera caught who it was for only a minute but got all the audio of it. One of them mentioned Jim at the beginning."

"Laura is in critical, but stable condition right now. The kick in the stomach did some damage internally, so she's in surgery right now so the doctors can see how bad it is. It'll be several days before they can work to repair her jaw though. The whole left side of her face is smashed in. Right now, I'm just praying she makes it through the first surgery. She's lost a lot of blood and is just broken. The minor injury was a possible broken arm when she got knocked to the ground. Why, Miss Peg? Why can't these guys just leave her alone? Jim will probably have charges against him because of it. More years added to his sentence, if the Sheriff has anything to say about it. He saw Laura's video and feels Jim is totally to blame. I just don't understand."

Miss Peg: "I am so sorry, Elizabeth. James holds a grudge for a long time. He is to blame completely for being in jail. His friends have always been loyal to one another. I hate to think he is behind this, but, if he is, then he should get a stiffer punishment than he now has. You said the Sheriff knows who did this? Will you tell me?"

"Elizabeth: "I don't want to put anything more on your shoulders right now. I think you know, anyway. I don't even want to say their names. Mrs. Walker's German shepherd got hold of one of them though and I guess he tore up his arm pretty good. He'll need it looked at. He won't leave the medical facility without the Sheriff right there. The Sheriff is taking the video to the Prosecutor yet tonight. Hopefully, he can get an arrest warrant quickly to put these animals in jail. Laura is the gentlest person you would ever want to meet. Why anyone would do this still shocks me."

"On a different—well, maybe—better note, when Mom died, some of the staff took over Laura's cleaning jobs. You know that's the first thing she'll think about when she wakes up. Could you ask them for me if they'll take over again? I know they'll appreciate the extra money. The job may become a permanent thing. I don't know that she'll be able to do it at all for a long time. I'd like to see her not have to do that at all anymore. She has had to work way too hard for the last ten years. This isn't the way to do it, but she needs a break."

"I'm sorry to burden you with this, but Laura would be angry if I didn't come and tell you in person. I really need to get back to the hospital. Jeremiah is driving home from Chicago. I want to be at the hospital when he gets there. I'm worried about him driving but there was no other choice. Say a prayer for Laura, okay?"

Elizabeth hugged Miss Peg and left. She hoped her prayers were being answered, and that Laura made it through surgery.

Chapter 38

It's been a little over four hours since Elizabeth talked to Jeremiah when he walked into the ER. Elizabeth just ran to him and buried her face in his shoulder. It didn't take much for her to start crying at that point.

Elizabeth: "I knew you would push yourself to get here. I'm relieved you're here though. I'm about to chew my fingernails to the quick sitting here alone."

Jeremiah: "Anything from the doctor yet?"

Elizabeth: "Not yet. No news in this case is not good news. She's been in there for over three hours. I know too much medicine right now to think it's good that she's still in surgery. All we can do now is pray. To give you a heads up before you see her, the punch she took in the jaw pretty much pushed the entire left side of her face in. The EMTs had to completely wrap her head to just be able to move her. Her tongue was cut up; she's lost teeth. They can't do any surgery on her jaw though, for at least a couple of days. The surgery tonight is really putting a strain on her, as it is. The doctors need to make sure she'll tolerate some sort of breathing tube. She is a mess right now. You just needed to know some of that."

"Sheriff Stone has the partial video she had taken. I hope the Prosecutor got the arrest warrants for these guys. He said he would let me know as soon as he can get something done."

Just then the doors opened, and the doctor came out. He looked utterly spent. Dr. Joseph Reynolds was one of the best surgeons at St. Ignatius Medical Center.

Dr. Reynolds: (Looking around) "Miss Parker?"

Elizabeth: "Yes, this is my brother, Jeremiah. How is she?"

Dr. Reynolds: "She has lost a lot of blood. We managed to replace most of it. She's critical right now and not very stable. Her vitals are all over the map. There was a lot of internal damage. I know she was kicked, but wonder what kind of footwear her assailant was wearing. It was almost like her stomach was pushed out her back. Just as we figured, we had to remove her spleen. You can live without a spleen.

Unfortunately, we had to remove her uterus. It had completely ruptured. That's where most of the blood was coming from in her abdomen. Luckily the kick just missed her bladder. It's badly bruised, as was her kidney. That's why there is blood in her urine. They should heal relatively quickly. We'll push fluids to get the blood flushed through. We may need to give her more blood."

"As I said, the sad part is the loss of her uterus. She will never have any children of her own. We'll deal with that at another time though. Right now, the next forty-eight hours will be crucial. We've had to put in a tracheotomy tube since we couldn't put in a regular vent down her throat. The damage to her jaw just wouldn't allow it. (He shakes his head.) I always have to wonder why someone would do something like this to another human being. She's healthy though. Let's hope her body can fight through all of this."

"To combat any infection that might occur because things were moved around to where they don't belong, and I had my hands in her abdomen so much, I've put her on some pretty strong antibiotics. So, she has all sorts of things flowing into her body to help her fight her way back from this."

"She is sedated and will remain so until we can get her stable. It will help us better investigate all of her injuries. When she does wake up, she'll be in a lot of pain. The sedation right now is saving her from that. It'll be a while before we bring her out, just for that reason. Her head CT didn't show any bleeding or fractures beyond her jaw. She was unconscious when she came in, then put under for her surgery, so she's been out for quite a while. When she does wake up, she'll be pretty confused. We'll keep you informed as to how she is doing."

Elizabeth: "Can we see her? I really need to see her."

Dr. Reynolds: "Not tonight. It's better to wait until she's more stable. Her appearance and condition right now would be very upsetting. Let the nurses do their magic with her tonight. Go home, get something to eat, and get some sleep. Come back in the morning. You'll be able to see her then."

Chapter 39

Just as they were getting ready to leave, Sheriff Stone came in. He asked how Laura was doing, and Elizabeth explained it all to him. He looked down and shook his head.

Sheriff Stone: "Oh man, I hate to hear that. She's in good hands here though. The nurses here are the best."

"To keep you updated, all three men have been arrested. It didn't take much convincing once the Prosecutor and the Judge saw the video. If you can believe it, they all tried to deny it. They don't know about the video. It was laughable how hard they all tried to talk their way out of it. Each one went kicking and screaming that they didn't do anything. Well, they can scream all they want. They've each been charged with assault and attempted murder."

"The Prosecutor also will charge James Martin with conspiracy in both charges. These three jokers will spend tonight in jail and be arraigned in the morning. Considering the charges, the Prosecutor will ask that they be remanded. They need to be off the street."

"Next thing, the press has gotten hold of this. There are a bunch of reporters outside the ER door. Mr. Parker, is your car here?"

Jeremiah: "Yes, why?"

Sheriff: "Deputy Friend here will go get your car and bring it around to the side door so you can get out without being barraged with questions tonight. Somewhere along the line, you may want to talk to the reporters, but tonight might not be the time. We'll get you out of here safely so you can go home safely. I'll send one of my deputies to take your car home, Miss Parker, if you'll give me your car keys. You deserve some peace tonight. This will get ugly before it's all over."

Elizabeth: "Thank you, Sheriff, you have been very kind. You're right; we do need some peace tonight. We can't see Laura tonight. The nurses need to care for her and do things we shouldn't see. It'll probably be a nightmare to get here tomorrow. Do you need us in court tomorrow?"

Sheriff: "No, I'll come and tell you what happens. You take care of your family."

Jeremiah: "Thanks, Sheriff. We'll talk to you tomorrow."

The Sheriff directed them to the side door where Deputy Friend had brought Jeremiah's car. They were able to get out of the parking lot without being seen by the reporters.

Laura's attack was on the late local news that night. The main reason was because three rich young men had been arrested and were sitting in jail. The fact that Laura was lying in a hospital bed fighting for her life took a back seat.

Chapter 40

There were a lot of reporters outside the hospital the following day when Elizabeth and Jeremiah got there to see Laura. After the news report last night, they decided to talk to the media. The wrong people were getting the attention. Jeremiah chose to set them straight.

Jeremiah: "Ladies and Gentlemen of the press, if you quiet down for a minute, my sister and I have chosen to make a statement. (Everyone quieted down.) Last evening when our sister, Laura, was standing in our front yard, she was attacked by three privileged men who felt that they didn't do anything wrong. I won't go into detail because I can't due to the Sheriff's investigation. I repeat, she was minding her own business, standing in our front yard. Right now she is lying in a bed in ICU, fighting for her life. The three rich men beat her without any provocation. Only they know the reason why."

"She has had to undergo a five-hour surgery to just save her life. The doctors have her sedated to keep her relaxed, so she can heal. She'll need many more surgeries in the future to survive. I'm not going to go into her injuries right now. We're just thankful she has made it this far. It'll be a long road to recovery for her. And why? Only these three men have the answer to that. I'm sure there are reporters at the courthouse right now trying to get some answers. I doubt these cowards will admit to anything though."

"Right now I'm just asking you all to let us have some privacy so we have the strength for Laura. We ask you all for your prayers. Like our mother, Laura is a big believer in the power of prayer. Whether you know Laura or not, believe in prayer or not, this is all we ask. Thank you for your time."

The reporters started throwing out questions, but Jeremiah just directed Elizabeth into the hospital. Thank goodness for the hospital security. They held off the throng that tried to follow them in.

Once upstairs, they were finally able to see Laura. It seemed like every type of machine available was in her room, monitoring everything. A large bandage covered her jaw and wrapped around her head to hold her jaw in place. The nurses had braided her long brown hair to keep it out of the way. There was bruising over her entire face; the left side was swollen. There was a tracheotomy tube attached to a machine doing most of her breathing for her. Her right arm was propped up on a pillow; a cast covered the entire arm. An IV in her left arm had several bags of fluids flowing into it, one of them blood.

You could hear the machine that was hooked to her mattress. It inflated different parts of the mattress to prevent any pressure on any area. Laura seemed so tiny lying in that bed. Every effort had been made to keep her comfortable—not that she was aware of any of it right now. After they had been there only a few minutes, the doctor walked in.

Dr. Reynolds: "Good morning. She's holding her own. Her vital signs evened out overnight. Her blood pressure is still elevated but not dangerous. We cannot know how much pain she still could be feeling. That could be a reason for her elevated blood pressure. We'll leave her on the vent for at least another twenty-four hours. After the twenty-four hours, we'll start to wean her off it. Hopefully, she'll be able to breathe on her own in a couple of days. Blood tests show her volume is back up, so this will be the last bag of blood we'll give her. The antibiotics though will go for a couple of days. Considering all she's been through, it looks like she will pull through."

The nurse walked in to check machines and bandages. She lifted the left side of Laura's gown and got a look of concern on her face.

Nurse: "Doctor, have you seen this large bruise on her side? I don't think it was here last night."

The doctor went to the left side of the bed, pressed his hands on the bruising, and frowned.

Dr. Reynolds: "Call X-ray and have them bring the portable in here. With all that was wrong, we may have missed some broken ribs. Let's check to make sure. I don't want to move her around only to have a rib puncture a lung."

The nurse left and the doctor started checking her further. Thankfully he didn't find anything else. The X-ray technician came into the room with the portable X-ray machine. Elizabeth and Jeremiah left the room with the doctor and the nurse. A few minutes later, the technician called the doctor back—everyone followed him.

Dr. Reynolds: "Yup, there are at least three broken ribs. By the bruising and the number, it looks like she got kicked. I don't see any other breaks though. We'll bind her chest above the incision. I think we can manipulate the ribs to heal correctly. Nurse, can you get me some long gauze bandages and the help of two other people? Now that we know about the ribs, let's get them taken care of as to not cause her any more pain when we bring her out of sedation. Miss Parker, Mr. Parker, this will take a couple of hours. It would be best if you weren't in the room. Four people in this room is pushing it. Why don't you go to the cafeteria and get some coffee? She'll be all settled back in a couple of hours. The nurse has your phone number. She can call you when we're done."

They did go down to the cafeteria. Neither of them felt like eating anything. Coffee was enough. While they were sitting there, Sheriff Stone called Elizabeth. It was after 1 p.m. She figured it had something to do with the arraignment so she put it on speaker.

Sheriff: "All four men have had their first day in court. Jim Martin was there by video. He did the most complaining. He's probably pissed that his name was even mentioned. Derek's right arm was heavily bandaged where Mrs. Walker's dog got hold of him. There were photographers everywhere, so their faces will be plastered on all forms of media tonight. Matt, Derek, and Andrew were charged with assault and attempted murder, held without bail. James was charged with conspiracy on both counts. He'll be put in solitary until their trials. We'll have to see if they're tried together or separately. I figured you would want to hear right away. How is Laura doing this morning?"

Jeremiah: "She's stable but still critical Her blood pressure is still up, but the doctor said it is to be expected. They found bruising on her left side this morning that wasn't there last night. X-rays showed three broken ribs. Sheriff, it looks like one of them kicked her in the side, besides just the stomach. The doctor will keep her sedated. He's afraid she wouldn't be able to deal with the pain she'll be in once she wakes up. We aren't in her room because they're binding her ribs so they heal properly. She's still on the vent. They'll try and wean her off in a couple of days. If I could get my hands on just one of those guys they would regret ever knowing my sister's name."

Sheriff: "I know how you feel right now. Doing that would probably make you feel a little better, but being the nonviolent person you are, maybe not. I'll keep you up to date on what's going on here. Please don't leave the hospital though without letting me know first. I'll make sure you'll have security if you need it."

Elizabeth: "Thank you, Sheriff. We appreciate all you've done. By the way, we got stopped outside the hospital this morning. We did give a short statement to the press but didn't get specific. Those jerks were headliners on the news last night. We only wanted everyone to know the truth. With any luck now, the press will get the story straight. We're headed back up to Laura. We'll talk to you later, Sheriff, thank you."

Sheriff: "Yes, I know. It was on the news at noon. You guys did very well. You were very concise and gave only the information needed to shut down the press. Maybe now they'll leave you alone."

On the way back to Laura's room Elizabeth remembered that she hadn't called her Aunt Connie. She would be devastated if something worse had happened and they didn't notify her. She needed to call Miss Peg, too, and let her know how Laura was doing.

Elizabeth stopped cold in her tracks. She was about the same age Laura was when their mom died. Now she understood better the rough time Laura had to be going through then. It made her heart hurt even more.

Chapter 41

Time seemed to creep by. Laura got a little stronger every day. Miss Peg came by every day to see how Laura was doing and to check on Elizabeth and Jeremiah. She couldn't stop apologizing for Jim's involvement in this. She was angry and upset that he had encouraged this kind of behavior. She still couldn't believe that he still carried this much anger, anger that didn't make any sense.

Four days after the attack, they were able to take her off the vent. She was breathing well through her tracheotomy tube. Her blood pressure also evened out. It seemed the binding of her ribs solved that problem.

The doctors had started lightening her sedation. So far she seemed to tolerate the lighter sedation. What the doctors worried about was her level of pain. They were evaluating her hour by hour. Any sign of agitation would mean she was feeling the pain from her injuries. If that started, they would increase her sedation again. Doctors don't like leaving someone in a medical coma like this. It was a wait and see situation.

Elizabeth and Jeremiah were torn about what they should do daily. They both had jobs and ongoing schooling. They could take a leave of absence from either of their jobs, but their schooling was a different matter. Jeremiah was scheduled to leave for France for his fellowship in six weeks. If he didn't go, he would lose the opportunity entirely. His was so torn. This was important to his future, but he didn't want to leave Laura for that long. He didn't want to put this all on Elizabeth's shoulders.

Elizabeth: "If you don't go and Laura finds out, she will never forgive herself. Our success means more to her than it does to us. Just plan on going. It's still six weeks away. We don't know how she'll be doing in that time. I've read that talking to someone in her condition helps them to heal. We'll just spend the time before you go to encourage her. She is very strong-willed. Give her some credit. She'll fight her way back from this faster than either one of us could imagine. You have to go. We can talk every day so you know how she's doing."

Jeremiah: "I don't know. She's my sister, too. You shouldn't have to be responsible for all her care by yourself. You have a life, too. I don't know if I'll be able to keep my mind on my work with her in this condition anyway."

Elizabeth: "That's just it. Chances are she'll be a lot better by the time you leave. Just plan on going. If she gets worse, you can always cancel, but, for right now stay on track with your plans. If she finds out you don't go because of her, she'll get out of that bed and kick your butt and you know it."

Jeremiah: "Okay! Okay! I give up. You two have always pushed me to do better. I guess I shouldn't expect anything different now. We'll just have to convince her to get better a lot quicker."

Elizabeth: "Good, now let's go talk to our sister and remind her she wouldn't let us give up. We won't give up on her either."

Chapter 42

In the courtroom downtown, two weeks after the attack a lawyer was still trying to get his clients out on bail until they went to trial for what the three men were claiming was a lie. They didn't know, yet, that the Prosecutor and a Judge had seen the video Laura had taken the day they attacked her. Each side, prosecution and defense, were just putting their cases together.

All three defendants were led into court, shackled. Each wore an expensive tailored suit, and their hair was neatly combed. Each wore a look of contempt on their face.

Matt Roman, dark hair, 265 pounds, six-foot-three, led the group.

Derek Sanders, blond hair, 289 pounds, six-foot-five, came next. His right arm was still bandaged from where Zeus had grabbed him.

Andrew Cassidy came last. His auburn hair was pulled into a ponytail. At 230 pounds and six-foot-one, he was the "smallest" of the group.

Right now all three men were being represented together by the same lawyer, Edward Bishop, the same lawyer for James Martin. Bishop figured he could defend all four men and get them all released—well, not James but the other three. The fact that the three men came from the wealthiest families in town didn't hurt, either. He made a nice amount of money from James Martin, and he didn't even win that case. Three clients all at once should bring him a nice payday, even if he didn't get anything from James. He was working on all of them being tried at the same time. One trial—three paychecks. Nice work if you can get it. The first thing he needed to do was get them out on bail. That was today's job.

Edward Bishop: "Your Honor, good morning. We're here today I hope to finally get a bail amount set for my clients. There is no reason they should sit in jail until we hold this sham of a trial. They all have jobs and have no criminal records. They deny all the charges as they say they were all the way across town at the time this woman was attacked. Her family was just trying to continue to get them to pay for the death of their father. So, Your Honor, I request a reasonable bail so they can again be productive members of our society. Thank you."

Lenny Jacobs: "Your Honor, you and I both know the reason Matt, Derek, and Andrew cannot be out on bail. They are a danger to others. Obviously, they don't agree with that. Miss Parker was the reason you lost your money tree. There is evidence that shows the reason you should spend the rest of your lives behind bars. Matt, what do you weigh?"

Matt: "Two sixty-five."

Jacobs: "How tall are you?"

Matt: "Six-three."

Jacobs: "Do you know how tall Miss Parker is? Five-one. Any idea what she weighs? A hundred seven pounds soaking wet. Matt, you are more than double her weight."

"I'm not going to go through all of this in a preliminary bail hearing. I just want you all to think of the discrepancy before you try and deny your actions."

"So, Your Honor, I believe this trial should be held off at least until the victim can be present to see the outcome. Right now, she's in a medically induced coma.

She would not be able to deal with the pain of all her injuries otherwise. And, since she cannot speak of the atrocities borne on her, I don't think the defendants should speak either. Miss Parker is, in essence, tied to a bed—unable to go out and do her normal duties. At this time, she is lying in that bed, fighting for her life. I'm sure if she was conscious, she'd tell you she'd rather be somewhere else. Since she has no freedom at this time, I don't feel these defendants deserve any freedom. I request they remain in jail until Miss Parker is able to speak and tell us what happened. These three should not be out partying while Miss Parker can't even move. Any bail will allow them to skip your jurisdiction, Your Honor. Prosecution rests."

With that, he sat down and waited for the Judge to make his decision.

Judge Matthews: "Mr. Jacobs, can you give me a timeline of when Miss Parker will be available? Two weeks, three weeks, a month?"

Jacobs: "No, Your Honor. As I said, she's in a medically induced coma right now. It's been touch and go for the last week. She barely made it through the first surgery. The doctors want her more stable before they attempt the twelve-plus hours it will take to repair her shattered jaw."

Judge: "Okay, I'm going to set a date for trial without her. It sounds like she won't be able to testify for a while. Mr. Jacobs, have you shown the video to the defense yet?"

Bishop: "WAIT—WAIT....What video? I haven't seen any video. I didn't even know one existed. Your Honor, I object to all of this. The Prosecutor obviously hasn't turned over all the discovery in this case."

Jacobs: "No, I haven't. I'll be honest, I wanted your clients to think they will skate on these charges. Your Honor, I will turn the tape over to the defense along with witness statements, the hospital report, and all evidence gathered from the defendants' homes as soon as you set a date. I didn't want them to concoct some story among themselves."

Judge: "Okay, I'm going to set the trial date for Monday, June 28th. Mr. Jacobs, please make sure the defense has all discovery by the end of business today. Mr. Bishop, that will give you a couple weeks to work on your defense. Is that agreeable to everyone?"

Jacobs: "Yes, Your Honor."

Bishop: "Yes, Your Honor. That way my clients will be home to celebrate the 4th of July."

Judge: "Fine, the date is set. The defendants, however, will remain in jail until then. Court dismissed."

Jacobs gathered his papers and was leaving the courtroom when he was stopped by Bishop.

Bishop: "Why wasn't I told there was a video connected to this case?"

Jacobs: "Because you didn't need to know until I had to turn over discovery. I don't know how to tell you, Ed, but I have an open and shut case because of the video. Your entitled clients will have no recourse after a jury sees it. And, if you're a decent human being, it'll make you sick. It did me. A messenger will have all of this to you this afternoon."

With that he turned on his heels and left, leaving Ed Bishop wondering how bad it could be.

Chapter 43

After she was a week off the vent and breathing well on her own, the doctors felt Laura could tolerate the surgery to repair her jaw. Her ribs are well-aligned and healing. The abdominal incision was healing. Blood work showed there was no infection anywhere. The doctors wanted her to wake up finally. Her jaw surgery could be stopped at any time if her vitals started to bounce around again. They felt it didn't need to be held off any longer. They didn't want the jaw to heal improperly.

At 6 a.m., Thursday, June 10, three weeks after the attack, Laura was wheeled into surgery to have her shattered jaw repaired. It was time for this.

Elizabeth and Jeremiah were there to encourage her to "hang tough." They didn't know how much she heard, but they kept talking to her anyway. They notified the congregation at the church of her surgery. There was a small group of parishioners in the surgery waiting room, holding a small prayer vigil. Laura was getting help from all bases. If she knew the prayers were being said, she would have felt even better.

Twelve hours…thirteen hours…fourteen and a half hours. The marathon surgery was completed. The doctor came out and told them that she had tolerated the procedure really well, considering all that had been happening to her. This surgery was not the end by any means for Laura. Right now, they had what was a jigsaw puzzle of bones mainly moved back to where they belonged. Her face would be more swollen now than it had been. Her tongue had been badly cut so it was stitched where it could be. The bandaging on her face now was to cover the surgery instead of supporting her jaw. There were now wires and pins holding her jaw together. Somewhere in the future, there would be more surgeries to continue to repair the damage, and she'd have to have a denture made so she had teeth on that jaw. Teeth weren't a priority though. She wouldn't be eating anything for a while. Yesterday, before the doctors were sure she would have the surgery, the doctors had a feeding tube placed. Just the IV solutions weren't enough to sustain her. She had started losing weight. The high-calorie formula would help her body heal much better. She needed every calorie she could get.

After the surgery, it was decided that Laura should be allowed to wake up completely. It was unsure how long that would take. There was a nurse by her side constantly. They were monitoring every movement, and level of consciousness. Elizabeth and Jeremiah never left her side. As while she was in her coma, they talked to her. They wanted her to know she wasn't alone. Elizabeth even explained to her all that was going on. If she were aware of Elizabeth, Laura hopefully wouldn't be afraid of where she was and why when she woke up. Either Elizabeth or Jeremiah was holding her hand. They wanted to know right away if she was responding.

She was taking her time waking up. This worried everyone. There was no sign from the beginning that she had any brain damage, but now they were wondering.

A little after four hours after the surgery, Laura's eyes just popped open. Fear showed in her eyes. Elizabeth was right there when this happened.

Elizabeth: "It's okay, Laura. We're here. I know you don't know what's going on, but trust me—you're okay. Jeremiah and I are here with you. Don't move, don't try to talk. Look at me—look at me. We'll take this one step at a time. First, are you in any pain? Stop and think so you know if you hurt anywhere. If you hurt anywhere, blink your eyes once for me. Now relax and think."

Laura was staring at Elizabeth. She took a deep breath and shook her head "no." She tried to speak but realized she couldn't. Her confusion was understandable. She tried to move around but was too weak to do anything. She did lift her arms a little and just looked confused that one had a cast, and the other was wrapped to protect an IV. Jeremiah held her hand while Elizabeth started to explain.

Elizabeth: "I don't know how much you remember, but you were attacked by three of Jim Martin's friends. One of them hit you and knocked you out. That's why all of this that you're seeing doesn't make sense to you right now."

The look in her eyes showed that she was thinking and trying to remember but didn't.

Elizabeth: "I'm not going to go into all the details but they messed you up pretty bad. Mrs. Walker's dog, Zeus, attacked one of them before they were able to do more than they did...I still need to take him a steak. (Chuckle.) He really let him have it."

At this point, Elizabeth was struggling so Jeremiah took over.

Jeremiah: "First of all, you've been in a medically induced coma for three weeks. In that time, you've had two surgeries. It's the one you just had that was the longest. The doctor felt though that it was time to let you wake up. Today's surgery was to repair your broken jaw. Whoever hit you did so with such force that he shattered the left side of your face."

Laura looked shocked at what Jeremiah had just told her. She tried to lift her left hand to feel her face but didn't have the strength yet. She started to cry.

Jeremiah: "Hold on, no crying. It'll be fine. The doctor who did the surgery is top-notch. You're probably going to start feeling some—well— discomfort, once the sedation completely wears off. Now isn't the time to go through all that happened that day or since. You'll heal and be good as new in no time."

Just then, Dr. Reynolds walked in. The nurse called him as soon as Laura woke up. He was smiling but still looked concerned.

Elizabeth: "Dr. Reynolds, we told Laura a *little* of what has happened, not all the details. She knows about the surgery she had today. I asked her if she was in any pain, and she shook her head 'no.'"

Dr. Reynolds: "That's fine. When she's fully awake, we'll go into more details. Okay, Laura? Well, look at that. This is the first time I've seen your eyes open. How did I know they would be a beautiful blue?"

Laura obviously was trying to smile—her eyes showed it. She stared at him though, wanting more answers than anyone was willing to give.

Dr. Reynolds: "Okay, Laura, I'm going to tell you a little more to avoid any surprises. Your brother and sister are trying to protect you, which is understandable, but you need to know a few things. I'm sorry, guys, I'm not going to go into details, but, she needs to know some things. If we don't say anything, she'll be more afraid of not knowing."

"Laura, when you came in, you were bruised pretty badly in your abdomen. X-rays showed there was excess fluid, so we operated and removed it. That's all you need to know now because you may experience some pain in your stomach and along the incision. We need to see if you're hurting so we can relieve your discomfort. We'll go into more detail later. Oh, and when you fell, you landed on your right arm and broke it—thus the cast. That's all we'll say right now. Your brain is pretty foggy right now, so that is enough for you to process. If you have any pain at all, call the nurse. I have ordered a mild pain medicine because I don't know how you will tolerate anything too strong. Right now, you have a feeding tube so we can get some calories in you. You need to start to build back your strength but slowly. The main thing is that I don't want you hurting. Any questions, anyone?"

Laura moved her left arm enough to point to her breathing tube.

Dr. Reynolds: "Oh, yes, that. Right now, I doubt you have any feeling in your mouth or tongue. We put in a nerve block to avoid some of the pain. It's numb, in other words. You may not be able to breathe right now, through your mouth, or your nose. We'll keep that in until you start to heal, and we're sure your throat won't block your airway. I'm sure you have plenty you want to say, but right now, let's concern ourselves with you breathing easily, okay?"

Laura shook her head "yes." She wasn't happy with the decision, you could tell, but accepted it nonetheless.

Elizabeth followed Dr. Reynolds out into the hall.

Elizabeth: "Thank you for not telling her everything. She's going to have trouble enough with the truth, but I don't want her upset about it right now."

Dr. Reynolds: "The full extent of her injuries will come out eventually, but there is no need to tell her right now. It isn't something she should worry about. She's pretty confused about all of this as it is. Like I told her, I just don't want her in a lot of pain. I have a suggestion. Get a computer tablet with a large keyboard. That will help her communicate with you. I've seen that work with other patients. She can hold a stylus in her left hand and type what she needs to say. Just don't treat her like she shouldn't know something. Stall, but don't lie to her. I have a feeling she'll see right through your lying anyway. She's fought back from the worst of this.

She needs our help to fight even more. I'll see her tomorrow. If she needs anything in the meantime the nurse will call me and I'll handle it immediately. She's obviously a very strong woman—we just need to help her pull through the rest of this. Good night."

Elizabeth: "Thank you, Doctor. We more than appreciate all you have done for her. Good night."

With that, Elizabeth put a smile on her face and walked back into Laura's room.

Elizabeth: "I am happy to see you awake. We're going to leave though. The nurses are kicking us out. You need some normal sleep. I'll put the call light in your hand so you can call the nurse if you need something. I'm going to buy a small tablet or something similar in the morning. You'll be able to type questions for us or the nurses. We'll see you in the morning. I love you, Laura."

Jeremiah: "Love you, Sis. We'll be back in the morning. Get some sleep and use that call light all you need to."

With that, they left, holding hands. When the elevator doors closed, they both broke down and just held on to each other and cried. Laura was going to make it.

When they got home, Elizabeth called Sheriff Stone and told him Laura was awake. She told him Laura wasn't aware of the extent of her injuries, and preferred it was left like that for right now. The Sheriff agreed. He'd go see Laura tomorrow when Elizabeth and Jeremiah were there. He needed to inform the Prosecutor that she was awake. In his heart he was glad he wasn't the one to tell Laura how badly she had been hurt.

Chapter 44

On the way to see Laura the morning after her surgery, Elizabeth and Jeremiah stopped at an electronics store to pick up a computer tablet like Dr. Reynolds had suggested. The staff assisted them in finding one that had a large keyboard she could use either with her fingers or a stylus. When told why they needed the tablet, the store manager cut the price drastically. He'd heard about Laura and wanted to help if he could. This was the way he could. That's just the way people in Kester were. Most of them were kind and generous. This proved it.

They were both anxious when they walked into Laura's room. They didn't know what to expect. To their surprise she was up, sitting in a chair. One of the nurses was in there making her bed. If Laura could speak, she would probably be telling her how to do it correctly by now. You could see in her eyes that she was happy to see the twins. They each carefully gave her a hug and sat down.

On the way to the hospital they had plugged the tablet into the charger in the car so she could use it right away. She was right-handed but had no trouble using her left hand to type on the keyboard. She looked happy that she could now communicate with everyone.

She had questions: What was today's date? How long had she been out? Most importantly, she wanted to know the extent of her injuries. She was starting to have pain in her stomach, and she wanted to know why.

Laura: (Typing) "I'm not stupid. Tell me why I hurt so much in my stomach if they only had to remove the fluid."

About that time, Dr. Reynolds walked in. Elizabeth let out a sigh of relief that she didn't have to answer that right away.

Dr. Reynolds: "Well, good morning, Blue Eyes. Look at you. I told the nurses they could get you up in a chair, but I didn't think they would do it so quickly. You need to rebuild your strength, so the first step was to get you out of that bed. The second step will be to get you out of ICU and to a regular floor. They have more ability to get you up and moving around again. Except for your broken arm, there are no broken bones and no reason you can't get up, with assistance for now, and start walking around. You're pretty weak so we'll start slow. Any questions?"

Laura nodded, though with some difficulty.

Dr. Reynolds: "Okay, Laura. I see your sister took my suggestion and got you a tablet so you can talk. What is your question?

Laura: (Typing) "Why does my stomach hurt so bad?"

Dr. Reynolds looked at the question and got a pained look on his face. He looked at Elizabeth and Jeremiah. Elizabeth didn't say anything, just shook her head "yes" and said that it was okay to tell Laura the truth.

Jeremiah got up from his chair so Dr. Reynolds could sit down to talk to Laura without her straining to look up at him. He sat there for a minute to carefully choose his words. This would not be an easy answer.

Dr. Reynolds: "During your attack it appears you were kicked twice, once in the ribs resulting in three broken ribs. They were pressing on your lungs, making it difficult to breathe. That's why you are bound around your chest."

He was stalling—she could tell. She took her left hand and slapped her thigh to get his attention. When he looked at her, he saw the anger on her face. She pointed to her stomach. She was getting impatient.

Dr. Reynolds: "Okay, this is the difficult part. (Pause.) When you were kicked, with what kind of shoe, I don't know, a couple of your organs were ruptured. The fluid in your abdomen was blood."

Laura was looking at him very intently at this point.

Dr Reynolds: "Thankfully, he kicked you off to the side enough that he just bruised your kidney and bladder. We were worried about where the blood was coming from because there was blood in your urine. Your spleen was shattered, so we removed that first....You can live very well without a spleen. Unfortunately though your uterus was severely torn and shredded. We couldn't repair it. We had to remove it along with your tubes and ovaries. I'm sorry, Laura. There was just no way we could save it, even though we really tried. That's why your stomach hurts. We had to do a lot of poking around to first try and repair it, then remove all of it since it couldn't be repaired. At that point, you had lost a lot of blood. The decision had been made for us. That was all we could do to stop the bleeding and save your life."

The look on Laura's face was utter disbelief. If she could, she probably would have been screaming right now. The tears started flowing. Elizabeth and Jeremiah got down next to her and held onto her. She had been denied the opportunity of having any children. The twins were well on their way to doing what they'd always dreamed of doing. She was looking forward to moving on, too. She had hoped to still get married and have a family. Now all of that was gone. After the realization sank in, the look of anger took over.

Laura: (She typed) "THOSE ASSHOLES HAVE TO PAY FOR THIS!"

One thing you never heard from Laura was curse words. This statement was a complete about face of who she was. It hurt everyone to see her hurting so much that she had resorted to this.

Elizabeth: "We were really hoping to hold off having to tell you this until you were stronger but knew, if you asked, we couldn't lie to you. Now that you know the truth, at least you can understand why you are hurting. Not much consolation, I know. We still have a lot to tell you."

The nurse came in and saw the looks on everyone's faces. Confused she asked if everything was okay.

Nurse: "Miss Parker, are you in any pain? Can I get you anything?"

Laura: (Types) "No, thank you."

Nurse: "I came in to tell you we are ready to move you to a different room. Are you ready?"

Jeremiah: "That's a good idea. Let's do that now. We'll let everything kinda sink in a little. Let the nurses get you settled in your new room and then we'll talk more. Is that okay, Laura?"

Laura still had a look of anger and pain in her eyes. These expressions alone caused her pain in her face due to her injuries. She looked at her brother and sister with tears still streaming down her face. She just nodded.

Jeremiah: "Okay, good. Do we need to leave or anything so you can move her?"

Nurse: "I just need to see that she's okay to move. I want to check her vitals and make sure she isn't too dizzy to make the trip. Miss Parker, are you at all light-headed? Do you need to go back to bed for a bit before we take you to your other room?"

With tears still flowing, she looked at the nurse and just shook her head.

The nurse said she wanted to clean her up and change her gown before she moved her so everyone left her room.

Dr. Reynolds: "I'm sorry I had to tell her like that. There was no way to bluff our way through that. That was the one thing I was dreading. From what I understand she is the one that raised you two."

Elizabeth: "Yes. Our dad was killed ten years ago, and our mom died seven or so years ago. Laura just took over. She wasn't about to let us go into foster care. She was only twenty-one. We've put her through a lot during the last years—you know, teenager stuff—but she never once complained. She always laughed that after raising us, she didn't want to start with a baby. You can see that was all bluster. I'm sure deep down, she wanted to be a mom to her own children. Now that she knows that's all been taken away I'm sure the devastation she's feeling is something none of us can understand. But, thank you, Doctor, for telling her as gently as you did."

Dr. Reynolds: "I would have preferred not to have to tell her at all, but she's crafty. She backed me into a corner. I didn't have any recourse. I'll go and let you and the nurses get her settled into her new room. I'll check on her later."

Chapter 45

After Laura was moved to a room on the medical floor she became withdrawn. She was getting stronger by the day, but had no joy in that fact. When the nurses would go into her room they would find her staring outside and often times crying. She said she wasn't in any pain...just unhappy.

Her jaw was healing well. The doctor was able to start minimizing the dressing that was covering her face. Ten days after her facial surgery, the doctors evaluated her to remove her trach. They removed the stitches on her tongue. The swelling had gone down considerably. She was able to swallow without choking. They closed her trach and watched to see if she could breathe normally. For all of this, the doctor had put her under a light sedation. If she was breathing well, they could close up her throat right away. Little at a time, she would be able to get her voice back.

When she woke up, she was over the moon. She was starting to feel a little normal again. It was now that Jeremiah decided it was time to drop his bomb about France.

The twins spent some time, every day, at the hospital now that Laura was doing so much better. They could see she was stronger but still sad about the first surgery. They both were able to go back to work and not worry quite as much. The day after her trach was removed, they were there helping her get her voice back.

Jeremiah: "I have something to tell you, Laura. I've decided not to go to France next month. I don't want to leave you and Elizabeth right now. I don't know if I could keep my mind on my studies for six months, not knowing how you both are doing…Laura? Say something. Here's your best chance to have something to say."

Laura just sat there and stared at him. She raised her hand and crooked her finger to indicate she wanted Jeremiah to come closer. When he moved in, she raised her hand and smacked him in the head. The anger on her face was unmistakable. She struggled, but managed to let him know what she wanted to say.

Laura: (Stammering and with halted speech) "There is no way you aren't going to France. You have worked too hard to get to this point not to go…and…I have worked too hard to get you to this point. I am much better."

She had to stop to catch her breath and swallow, but she wasn't done with him.

Laura: "Elizabeth and I will be fine. I'm due to be discharged any day. You cannot use me to be the reason you don't finish your schooling. I won't allow it. I plan to kick your butt all the way to the airport if I have to. Elizabeth, did you know he was thinking about this?"

Elizabeth looked down at the floor and nodded.

After all of this attempt at talking Laura lost her breath and started coughing. That caused a different kind of pain. Her ribs were still healing, as was the incision in her abdomen. She wrapped her left arm around her waist as much as she could, but you could see she hurt badly right now.

Elizabeth got the nurse and she quickly grabbed the oxygen from the wall to help her breathe easier.

Once she was able to attempt to talk again, Laura started again.

Laura: (Still struggling but determined) "If you don't go...you lose. Do you know who wins? Jim Martin and his clown circus. All these years, he has been trying to beat us down. Don't let him win this time. Go to France and come back the winner. Please. Think of what Mom and Dad would tell you to do. They would tell you to let your sisters handle this here. You go to France and handle that."

"Their trial starts next week. They tried to beat us. So far, their money hasn't gotten them out of this. They took my babies away from me. They can't be allowed to take your dream away from you, too."

She had said all she could. She was having trouble catching her breath. She could just stare at Jeremiah. She was having trouble that he was even considering putting the brakes on his education and dreams. She couldn't be the reason he did that. She just shook her head. She looked at Jeremiah and just started crying. After all the years she worked so hard to get him where he was right now, and he was giving up. She waved them both away.

Laura: "Go home. I'm tired. I'm going to lie down."

With that she lay down and turned away from the twins. She felt very disappointed and whipped. The twins left.

When they came back the next day, Jeremiah's decision had changed.

Jeremiah: "Okay, Laura. I leave for France in about two weeks. I can't let you down. I'll do my best over there, I promise."

There were X-rays taken of Laura's right arm. The bone had healed. The cast would come off today. One more step before her discharge. She needed to do the swallow tests yet to see if the feeding tube could be removed. That was the last hurdle before discharge. It would be some time before she'd tolerate solid food but if she was swallowing okay, pureed food would sustain her. She just wanted to go home already.

Chapter 46

The trial started the next week. Mr. Jacobs had gotten his wish. Laura would be able to testify. Her speech right now was halting, and she needed to stop and just breathe occasionally. With still a broken jaw, she was struggling with the pronunciation of some words. She'd get through it though. Since Matt's punch knocked her out, she didn't remember the entire attack.

Sheriff Stone and Mr. Jacobs went to the hospital to see how well she was doing. Mr. Jacobs wanted to hear from her about what she remembered. He didn't need her to say much. She'd say a few things though about the aftermath of the attack resulting in the surgery that would forever change her life. The jury would hear exactly what those men took from her. This would all be after she identified her attackers. After that the jury would see the pictures taken right after the attack. Hospital personnel took pictures when she was brought in for reference. And then, there was the infamous tape Laura had inadvertently recorded. That was the one thing Mr. Jacobs really wanted the jury to hear and see.

It was chilling to see Matt come at her and hit her. The ugly look of anger on his face would make everyone cringe. Mr. Jacobs would again note the weight discrepancy. Any one of these men could easily have picked her up and thrown her. No matter how hard she would have tried, she was no match for their brute force. He'd make sure the jury saw that. What kind of threat did this tiny woman pose?

Two days after the Prosecutor and the Sheriff visited Laura in the hospital, she was discharged. It felt good to be home. All the beautiful flowers that had greeted her the last time she was home were all bloomed out. The short memory of that day came rushing at her. She hesitated when she got out of the car. Jeremiah was right there though to support her.

Mrs. Walker and her dogs were there to greet her. Laura got down and hugged both of them. She held Zeus a little longer, knowing he was the one to stop the attack. She shuttered to think what may have happened if he hadn't. The thought brought tears to her eyes. She hugged Mrs. Walker and just hung on.

Chapter 47

June 28. The courthouse was again a media circus. The people of Kester were shocked at what three privileged men had done to Laura Parker. The cult following of Jim Martin had gone too far.

Someone from the press had managed to sneak into the hospital and had gotten pictures of Laura right after the attack. It showed her bandaged head, cast on her arm, IV going. It was hard to tell who she was; her face was so bruised and swollen.

Bishop, the defense attorney, wasn't happy that the picture had been made public. He wasn't sure now if he could impanel an impartial jury.

At 8:50 a.m., the defendants were brought into the courtroom. All were dressed in their best suits, shoes shined, and hair styled. The Bailiffs removed their shackles and stood behind them. A video monitor had been set up next to the defense table. Jim Martin was on the screen. The four of them acted like it was old home week—talking and laughing with each other. It was like they had no idea just how horrible this situation was or how much trouble they were really in. You see, for some odd reason, Mr. Bishop never showed them the tape. He told them about it and said it wasn't good, but they never actually saw it. They were in for a surprise like everyone else.

9 a.m., on the dot.

Bailiff: "All rise. The Honorable Brandon Matthews presiding. (Pause.) Be seated."

Judge: "Good morning, everyone. I see today we pick a jury. Mr. Jacobs, are the people ready?"

Jacobs: "We are, Your Honor."

Judge: "Mr. Bishop, I see you have a full table over there plus, hello, Mr. Martin. Is the defense ready?"

Bishop: "Actually, no, Your Honor. The press has large pictures everywhere of the victim right after the alleged attack. I request a change of venue. I don't feel we can get an impartial jury here in Kester."

Judge: "I don't agree with you, Mr. Bishop. The people of Kester have always shown to be very impartial and follow the rule of law. If you remember, when Mr. Martin was before this court in the past, the jury asked for clarification on several matters before rendering their verdict. I feel the jury we impanel for this trial will do the same. I ask you again...don't make it three.... Is the defense ready?"

Bishop: "I guess as we'll ever be, Your Honor."

Judge: "Bailiff, will you bring in the first panel?"

The jury questioning went back and forth all morning. By lunch they only had four jurors selected. This was not going as well as the Judge had hoped.

Judge: "It is time for a lunch break. I hope we can do a little better this afternoon. We'll reconvene at 1:30 p.m. Court adjourned for now."

The Judge stood up and was gone before the Bailiff could make everyone rise.

It was decided that Laura wouldn't attend the jury selection. She wanted her appearance to be a surprise when the trial proceedings began. By not going, the defense could not say there was any undue influence on the selection of the jury.

At 1:30 p.m., the Bailiff got the courtroom in order as Judge Matthews entered, more shuffling feet as more potential jurors were brought in.

The proceeding went a little smoother in the afternoon. By 4:55 p.m., the other eight jurors and one alternate were selected. The Judge smiled and looked at his watch.

Judge Matthews: "Good work, people. We'll adjourn for the day and return at 9 a.m. tomorrow."

With that, he stood up and left the courtroom. The usual chatter went on before everyone left.

Miss Peg, Elizabeth, and Jeremiah again sat behind the Prosecutor. The three families of the other men sat behind the defense table. You could see the daggers they were shooting from their eyes at Miss Peg and the twins. Again it was as if they were to blame for their sons' trouble. Miss Peg had learned to ignore them. They may have had money—New Money—but Miss Peg was wealthy—Old Money. She could stare them down like nobody's business. She had taken the Parkers under her wing, so no one had better mess with them. Oh, those four tried, but it wasn't going to fly.

Chapter 48

When court proceeded on the 29th, the courthouse halls, steps, and courtroom were packed. Now, Judge Matthew had proven to be a no-nonsense judge. As with Jim Martin's trial, he let everyone know that there would be no disruptions. He had dealt with this group before. He knew how rowdy they could be. He had the solution for it this time.

Judge Matthews: "Bailiffs, I want you to position yourselves around the courtroom. I will not allow any disruptions. Regardless of who they are, you are instructed to remove that person and take them right to a holding cell. That includes the defendants. The emotions for this trial will run high. I won't have any outbursts. Both sides of the aisle will be allowed to present their case without any side comments. Now, if that is clear, are we ready to proceed?"

Mr. Jacobs: "Yes, Your Honor."

Mr. Bishop: "I renew my objection to having the trial held in this jurisdiction. Your Honor should not have had to make the statement you just did. I don't feel my clients will be judged fairly here."

Judge: "Okay, Mr. Bishop. That was strike three on this ruling. I should throw you out now as you are the one trying to unduly influence the jury. Any more statements like the one you just made, and you will be thrown off this case, and a public defender will take over. Do I make myself clear, Mr. Bishop? Your clients and their families need to reel you in right now. Just defend your clients."

Bishop: "Yes, Your Honor."

Judge: "Fine..Mr. Jacobs, you may proceed."

Jacobs: (Standing up and facing the jury) "Ladies and Gentlemen of the Jury, I will make this short so we can get to the meat of this trial. It is all pretty straightforward. The defendant on the screen, James Martin, is still holding a grudge because he is now sitting in prison for Obstruction of Justice and Accessory After the Fact in the Vehicular Manslaughter of David Parker, the victim's father in this case. The other three defendants, Matthew Roman, Derek Sanders, and Andrew Cassidy, have known him all their lives. James Martin has been the leader of the pack, so to speak, because the other three just followed him around. He had the money, and they liked to spend it. His anger spilled over to his three friends. So, when he obviously suggested they pay Laura Parker a not-so-friendly visit, they did as he asked. Miss Parker has had no dealing with Mr. Martin or his friends. She didn't provoke them to do the violent act they performed. You'll see, and hear the video that Miss Parker actually took accidentally. Even though the video part is short, the audio tells the rest of the story. The sad reason for all of this was money. None of them had access to it anymore because James Martin is behind bars. Miss Parker should not have had to pay for that reason though. Especially as much as she did."

Mr. Jacobs sat down. It was Mr. Bishop's turn.

Bishop: "If it pleases the court, I will hold my opening argument for a later date."

Judge: "That's fine. Mr. Jacobs, are you ready to call your first witness?"

Jacobs: "Yes, Your Honor. I call Mrs. Beatrice Walker to the stand."

Chapter 49

Beatrice Walker walked to the witness stand.

The Bailiff swore her in—with her hand on the Bible.

Bailiff: "Do you swear to tell the truth, the whole truth and nothing but the truth, so help you, God?"

Beatrice: "I do."

Bailiff: "Please state your name and address."

Beatrice: "Beatrice Walker, 52381 Sweet Spring Road, Kester, Illinois."

Bailiff: "Thank you."

Jacobs: "Mrs. Walker, how do you know Laura Parker?"

Beatrice: "Oh, the Parker family has lived across the road from me for about thirty years or better. I watched those children be born and grow up over there."

Jacobs: "Have you ever known them to be violent or disruptive in any way?"

Beatrice: "Oh, Heavens, no. The most I've heard from there is the children's laughter. They're older now, but when they were little, the laughter from there was contagious."

Jacobs: "So, on May 22nd of this year, when you heard yelling and screaming from the Parker residence, it was completely unusual?"

Beatrice: "Oh yes. Someone was very angry over there. You could hear it in their voices."

Jacobs: "Mrs. Walker, can you tell the court why you were out in your yard that day?"

Beatrice: "Well, it was about 3 p.m., on a Saturday. My dogs, Brutus and Zeus, let me know it was time to go out. Right before I opened the door, I saw a FedEx truck go down the side road. They deliver on Saturdays, you know. For some odd reason, neither of my dogs likes the FedEx trucks, so to avoid having to yell at them, I put them on their leashes. It meant they didn't completely have the run of the yard, but I had control of them when the truck went by."

Jacobs: "Go on, Mrs. Walker.

Beatrice: "I was walking down the driveway when I saw Laura pull into her driveway. She waved as she walked into the house. About a minute later, she came out and was using her phone to get pictures of the flowers out front of the house. They were especially beautiful this year. Everything was in full bloom. About the time she got halfway down the house, a big black pickup truck sped into her driveway, and three men got out."

Jacobs: "Mrs. Walker, have you ever seen those men at the Parker home before?"

Beatrice: "No, but I remember seeing the blond man in the courtroom at James Martin's trial."

Jacobs: "Mrs. Walker, do you see the men that got out of that big black pickup truck here in the courtroom?"

Beatrice: "Yes, they are sitting at that table beside the monitor with James Martin on it."

Jacobs: "Please let the record show that Mrs. Walker identified the defendants, Matthew Roman, Derek Sanders, and Andrew Cassidy. Now, Mrs. Walker, what drew your attention to what was going on across the road?"

Beatrice: "The men jumped out of the truck, and started yelling at Laura. I couldn't believe anyone would have a reason to yell at Laura. Then I saw the driver of the truck, the dark-haired man there at the table, swing and hit Laura. I couldn't believe what I saw. I was so shocked I kinda froze in my tracks. I was finally able to yell at them, 'What are you men doing?' All this time, Brutus and Zeus were barking and growling. They aren't easily agitated, but something caused them to get angry. I didn't see where Laura was at this point. I got worried, so I dropped the dogs' leashes and gave them the command to act. They had been pulling on the leashes, so I figured they knew something I couldn't see."

"Well, my dogs are guard dogs. You don't really want to mess with me or the Parkers. They were trained to protect me and those children after they lost their parents. Anyway, Brutus, my rottweiler, and Zeus, my king shepherd, took off to protect Laura. The men saw and heard them coming, so they ran to their truck as fast as they could. It wasn't quick enough for one of them though. Zeus got hold of his arm and hung on. The man was screaming to get him off. I was afraid they would run over him or something, so I gave Zeus the command to release. As soon as he did, they were speeding out of the driveway, and onto the road. I was sure the blond one was hurting because Zeus had him pretty firmly by the arm."

Jacobs: "Mrs. Walker, can you continue? What did you find when you got across the road? Where was Laura?"

Beatrice: (With a catch in her voice) "She was on the ground unconscious. Her face was badly distorted from where the man had hit her. She was barely breathing. I was afraid to even touch her. I didn't want to hurt her any more than she was. My poor Brutus just lay beside her, whining because he couldn't get a response from her. I grabbed my cell phone and called 911. I explained everything. I had to leave her for a couple of minutes to put the dogs up. If I hadn't, no one would have been able to get close to Laura. When I got back to her, I found her cell phone. The camera app was still open, so I closed it so I could call her sister, Elizabeth, and tell her what was going on. I was on the phone with her when I heard the sirens. I put both phones in my pocket. It only took the Sheriff and the ambulance a few minutes to get there but it seemed like forever. I just knelt down beside Laura and talked to her until everyone arrived."

"About ten minutes later, Elizabeth arrived at the house as EMTs were working on Laura. I handed her Laura's phone and asked her to check the camera app on it. I thought she might have taken a photo of the men who had attacked Laura. The look on Elizabeth's face was one of shock and disbelief. She showed the photo to the Sheriff. The sheriff's reaction was one of anger. It wasn't until the ambulance arrived at the hospital that they were able to transfer Laura."

Jacobs: "You said you saw the man who hit Laura. Did you see any of the other ones do anything else to her?"

Beatrice: "Oh, yes, I saw the blond one kick at her. I don't know if he connected or not though....Oh, by the way, young man, how is your arm?"

Bishop: "Your Honor!"

Judge: "Hmm, Mrs. Walker, please don't talk to any of the defendants."

Beatrice: (Smiling) "I'm sorry, Your Honor, but I couldn't resist."

Jacobs: "Thank you, Mrs. Walker. That was very informative. I have no further questions for this witness, Your Honor."

Judge: "Mr. Bishop, do you have any questions for this witness?"

Bishop: "Yes, Your Honor, thank you. Mrs. Walker, you said you gave your dogs a command to attack, is that right?"

Beatrice: "Yes, I did."

Bishop: "Why?"

Beatrice: "Actually, I couldn't hold them back had I wanted to. There were men around Laura that they didn't know, and I had just yelled at them. The dogs knew there was something wrong. They both are very intelligent and trained to notice trouble."

Bishop: "You gave them a specific command?"

Beatrice: "Yes."

Bishop: "Would I know you had given the command?"

Beatrice: "Probably not."

Bishop: "What was the command you gave them?"

Beatrice: "To attack."

Bishop: "But what was the actual command you gave?"

Beatrice: "The command words I chose are unusual enough that the dogs would only hear them if there was trouble."

Bishop: "And what are those commands?"

Beatrice: "I won't tell you. That's the idea of using an unusual word, so only the dogs know what I want."

Bishop: "Your Honor, Mrs. Walker used a command that my clients didn't know. I insist she tells us what those words are."

Judge: "Not going to happen, Mr. Bishop. All guard dogs are given command words that only their handlers know. That's the same in this case. I will not make her divulge the words. Move on or dismiss her."

Bishop: "I have no further questions of this witness, Your Honor."

Judge: "Fine, Mrs. Walker, you are dismissed."

Beatrice walked back to her seat but not before giving an angry look to all the defendants.

Jacobs: "I would like to call Dr. Joseph Reynolds to the stand at this time."

Bishop: "I object, Your Honor. Isn't anything he might have to say privileged?"

Jacobs: "Your honor, Miss Parker has okayed Dr. Reynolds to testify, in the narrow scope, of only the injuries on admission to the hospital. Not any subsequent treatment beyond that."

Judge: "Objection overruled. Dr. Reynolds, will you take the stand? You are only to testify about the condition Miss Parker was in when she came into the ER...not anything she may have had done after that. Is that understood?"

Dr. Reynolds: "Yes, Your Honor."

The Bailiff swore him in.

Jacobs: "Good morning, Doctor Reynolds. How long have you practiced medicine?"

Dr. Reynolds: "Just over twenty years. Most of it in the ER."

Jacobs: "I know you treated Laura Parker for her five weeks or so in the hospital, but we'll just focus on

Saturday, May 22nd, when she was brought in by ambulance. Can you start head-to-toe to describe her condition?"

Dr. Reynolds: "To put it bluntly, she was a train wreck. When I first saw her, I thought she had been in a car accident with a large vehicle. That's how severely we saw her injuries. I was shocked when I heard it was the result of a physical attack. I've treated a lot of domestic violence injuries but never something this severe."

At this point Matthew Roman thought it would be cute to chuckle quite loudly.

Judge: "Mr. Bishop, control your client, or I will have him removed from the courtroom."

Bishop: "I apologize, Your Honor, but I object. The doctor is exaggerating her injuries to make the Prosecutor's case."

Dr. Reynolds: "No, actually, I'm not. Miss Parker had been beaten severely. May I continue, Your Honor?"

Judge: "Yes, Doctor, please continue."

Dr. Reynolds: "The EMTs informed us that the victim had been struck to the ground, and that only her jaw had been shattered. At the time, the victim was breathing well and was beginning to struggle. Intubation was attempted; however, it was determined that this would not be a long-term solution. The jawbone had caused a severe cut in the tongue, which necessitated the use of a tube to keep the tongue from obstructing the airway. Gauze was applied to the jaw to stabilize it."

"The victim had been unconscious, and her right arm had been wrapped, and an X-ray revealed that the arm had been fractured. A full examination of her body showed abdominal bruising and swelling. There was some vaginal bleeding that we ascertained was not menstrual blood. Something else was going on in her abdomen. We started an IV for fluids and possibly blood and put her on a vent to make sure she was breathing without too much difficulty. Due to the bleeding and abdominal swelling, we decided to take her to surgery to see where the blood was coming from. At this point, we explained all of this to her sister. We were keeping a close eye on her vital signs. They were bouncing all over the place. Our main concern was to keep Miss Parker alive. Her body was fighting a lot.

That's the complete time in the ER that I'm allowed to discuss."

Jacobs: "Thank you, Doctor. That was very concise considering your limitations. No further questions."

Bishop: "Doctor, did anyone tell you who or what hit Miss Parker?"

Dr. Reynolds: "If someone did, I don't remember. That would not have made any impact on the care we gave to Miss Parker though. I am only there to repair the damage...not point fingers as to the cause for those injuries."

Bishop: "Thank you, Doctor. No further questions."

Judge: "Mr. Jacobs. Do you have any other witnesses?"

Jacobs: "I do, Your Honor. But it is close to lunch, so I wonder if we can continue with this this afternoon?"

Judge: "That sounds like a good idea. Court adjourned until 1:30 p.m."

The courtroom emptied, but not without a lot of chatter and dirty looks from the defendants.

Chapter 50

At 1:15 p.m., the jury and the defendants were back in the courtroom.

At 1:30 p.m., the Bailiff called the court to order, and Judge Matthews sat down.

Judge: "Mr. Jacobs, will you call your next witness?"

Jacobs: "Yes, Your Honor. I call Sheriff Mark Stone to the stand."

The Bailiff swore him in, and he sat down.

Jacobs: "Good afternoon, Sheriff Stone. How long have you served as sheriff of this county?"

Sheriff Stone: "Twenty-seven years."

Jacobs: "So it's reasonable to assume you've dealt with most residents from time to time?"

Sheriff: "Yes, I hate to admit it, but for one reason or other, I've had dealings with just about everyone in this county."

Jacobs: "On May 22nd of this year, did you have reason to go to the Parker residence at 52493 Sweet Spring Road?"

Sheriff: "Yes, unfortunately. I was answering a 911 call that someone there had been assaulted. I was told there was also an ambulance dispatched."

Jacobs: "Have you ever been to this address for anything like this before?"

Sheriff: "The last time I was there was to inform the family about the investigation into the death of David Parker. It was about ten years ago."

Jacobs: "Okay, Sheriff, what did you find when you got to this residence?"

Sheriff: (Hrmph.) "A young woman, Laura Parker, was on the ground in her front yard. She was lying on her right side—unconscious. The left side of her face had begun to swell, and her whole jaw was—well—

where it shouldn't be. A neighbor, Mrs. Walker, was sitting beside her. She told me she didn't want to touch her for fear of hurting her any further. The ambulance was right behind me. The EMTs got to work getting Miss Parker ready to transport. It took them a while because her jaw was so crumpled that they had to make sure it didn't move any further. They struggled and managed to get a breathing tube down her throat because she wasn't breathing well."

"Within minutes of my arrival, Miss Parker's sister, Elizabeth, arrived. I had to hold her back from going to her sister so the EMTs could do their job. Mrs. Walker pulled Elizabeth to the side to comfort her. That was when she gave her Miss Parker's phone. Elizabeth looked at it and brought it over to me. That's when I saw the video Miss Parker had taken of her attackers. I took Miss Parker's phone and sent the video to my phone to be used as evidence."

Jacobs: "Sheriff, when Mrs. Walker testified, she said that when you saw the video, you got an angry look on your face. Why was that?"

Sheriff: "Because I recognized the men right away. Along with Jim Martin, these men were like a large stone in my shoe. They've been in and out of trouble since they were teenagers. Their parents would bail them out of trouble, and they would be on to the next thing. I had hoped they had outgrown causing trouble, but I saw that day that their trouble making had only escalated. Three men, all over two hundred pounds each, decided it was a good idea to beat a hundred-pound woman—on the say-so of a buddy. I'll never understand people's motives."

Jacobs: "Sheriff, what did you do next?'

Sheriff: "I waited until Miss Parker was in the ambulance and on her way to the hospital. I talked to Elizabeth Parker for a few minutes before she headed to the hospital. I then took the video to show you, Mr. Jacobs, to get an arrest warrant for these three. You told me you would take it from there. Later that evening I went to the hospital to let Elizabeth Parker know what I had done. She told me that Laura was holding on so far and that she was in surgery."

"Within a couple of hours you had contacted me to arrest Matthew Roman, Derek Sanders, and Andrew Cassidy. I sent deputies out so we could arrest all three at once. I didn't want them calling each other to make up some story or evade arrest.."

Jacobs: "What kind of condition was Derek Sanders when you arrested him?"

Sheriff: "Whiny. He said a friend's dog had gotten carried away when they were playing and tore up his arm. He wanted to go to the hospital to have it taken care of before he went anywhere."

Jacobs: "And?"

Sheriff: "Oh, we took him to a clinic to have it looked at. He was handcuffed though and really complaining that he wanted to go to the real ER. I didn't figure he needed that extensive of treatment. Besides, I didn't want him anywhere near the Parkers in the hospital ER. Don't kid yourself; he received excellent care at the clinic."

Jacobs: "Oh. One more question, Sheriff. When was the last time you saw Laura Parker?"

Sheriff: "Actually, right in this courtroom when she made the Victim Impact Statement at James Martin's trial regarding the death of her father."

Jacobs: "James Martin didn't kill her father though, did he?"

Sheriff: "No, he just covered it up for years, causing that family undue hardships. That's why he's on a monitor from a prison instead of sitting next to his co-defendants."

Jacobs: "Thank you, Sheriff. Your witness."

Bishop: "Sheriff, so you didn't think Mr. Sanders deserved the care in a first-class trauma center?"

Sheriff: "He didn't need the trauma center. He needed the dog bites cleaned, a couple of stitches, and a clean dressing is all."

Bishop: "So, second-class treatment for someone who allegedly attacked someone?"

Sheriff: "There's nothing second class about the medical clinic where he was treated. It is one of the best in the state."

Bishop: "You had it in for my clients because you feel they had gotten away with things since they were teenagers?"

Sheriff: "That isn't what I said or meant. I said I was familiar with them since they were teenagers. Maybe if they had received some punishment for their activities as teenagers, they would have known that bad actions have consequences. They obviously never learned that."

Bishop: "How can we be sure that once you got hold of that tape, that you didn't doctor it to accuse my clients?"

Sheriff: "You've had the tape; you could have a forensic audiologist inspect the tape just as we did. I believe you have a copy of his report. I am law enforcement. I follow the law to the letter. I don't have to make up evidence. Your clients are guilty of the crime they have been charged with. They're trying to do what all four of them have done their whole life—

blame someone else for their deeds. It doesn't work here."

Bishop: "But you still could have added something to the tape anyway, right?"

Jacobs: "Your Honor, Mr. Bishop is trying to make this up as he's going."

Judge: "Move on, Mr. Bishop."

Bishop. "Fine, I have no further questions for this witness."

Judge: "You may step down, Sheriff. Mr. Jacobs, do you have any other witnesses?"

Jacobs: "Yes, Your Honor. However, to not unduly influence the jury, this witness is not in the gallery. The testimony will be time-consuming, so I wonder if we could stop here tonight and resume with this witness in the morning?"

Judge: "That sounds like a good idea. We'll break now and resume at 9 a.m. Court is adjourned."

Jacobs got up and turned to talk to Elizabeth and Jeremiah. They would go home and let Laura know what was going on. Laura was coming back in the morning to testify. They wanted to make sure she was going to be able to face her attackers.

Chapter 51

The jury, defendants, the Prosecutor, and the gallery were all seated at 8:45 a.m.

At 9 a.m., the Judge walked in.

Bailiff: "All rise. The Honorable Brandon Matthews presiding (Pause for judge to sit.) You may be seated."

Judge: "Are we ready to proceed?"

Bishop: "Yes, Your Honor."

Jacobs: "Yes, Your Honor."

Judge: "All right, Mr. Jacobs, you may call your next witness."

Jacobs: "Thank you, Your Honor. I now call Laura Parker to the stand."

It seemed everyone in the courtroom decided to talk at once. The Judge wasn't happy. He had to pound his gavel several times to quiet everyone down.

Judge: "I have made myself perfectly clear that I would not allow any outbursts from anyone in this courtroom. Bailiffs, any more outbursts like that, and you will clear the room. Okay, now we can proceed."

Elizabeth had walked out into the hall to be with Laura as she entered the courtroom. She had been in a sequestered room, so no one knew she was there. Elizabeth took her by the hand, and they walked through the door together.

The gasps from the room reverberated. Laura hesitated just inside the room when she heard everyone. Jeremiah got up from his seat and went to Laura. He took her hand, shook his head, nodded, and smiled at his sister. It seemed he gave her the added courage to go the rest of the way to the witness chair. The reason for all the gasps was that Laura chose not to wear any face covering when she walked into the courtroom. The left side of her face was still disfigured and there was a large red scar from her left ear around to the right side of her chin. There was a lot of swelling and redness on the left side of her face. You could still see the remainder of a black eye. She wanted a reaction from everyone. Let them all see what she was living through.

Even the Judge hadn't seen her. There was an honest shocked look on his face. The defendants just stared—no expressions at all. The jury was really impacted. A couple of women had their hands on their mouths. They looked like they were about to cry. This was the reaction the Prosecutor had hoped for. She probably didn't even have to say a word. Her appearance said it all.

The Bailiff swore her in with tears in his eyes.

Laura had had enough. She put the mask on her face that she brought with her. She didn't want everyone to see, in any way, how difficult it was for her to move her mouth to speak. The reaction was more than she expected. She was a little shaky.

Jacobs: "Good afternoon, Miss Parker. Do you feel well enough to be here today?"

Laura: "Yes. P-p-please, call me...Laura."

Jacobs: "Okay, Laura. We'll take this slow since I know you still have some trouble forming words.

"First, Laura, do you know the three men sitting at that table and the one on the screen?"

Laura: "Yes...unfortunately."

Bishop started to stand up, but the Judge waved him down.

Jacobs: "When and where was the last time you saw them? Take your time."

Laura: "Saturday, May 22nd, in my front yard. I know the exact date because I had just gotten home from a baby shower."

Jacobs: "Do you remember seeing Mrs. Walker and her dogs when you got home?"

Laura: (Smiling with her eyes) "Yes, I love those dogs and Mrs. Walker. She brings them out, and they run right to me. For as large as they are, they're really gentle."

Jacobs: "Would it surprise you to know they were far from gentle that day when they saw the defendants in your yard?"

Laura: "No, it wouldn't. I think I owe my life to Zeus, the king shepherd. These are about the best-trained dogs you'll ever see. They're trained like police dogs but to protect someone. Mrs. Walker had them trained to not only protect her but my family as well. They came across the road, to not play with me, but to protect me from what they obviously deemed was danger."

Jacobs: "I know you don't remember much, but can you take your time and tell us what you do remember about that day?"

Laura: (With obviously a pained look on her face) "I'll tell you what I do remember. When I pulled into the yard, I saw how beautiful all our flowers were across the front of the house. About fifteen years ago, my mom and my Aunt Connie planted azalea and rhododendron plants. This year they were huge and in full bloom. I decided to take a video of them and share it with my aunt. I knew she would love to see them. She doesn't live in Kester, so, she couldn't just come over to see them. It's been painful for her to come to the house anyway since my mom died."

"I was walking across the front of the house when I heard a vehicle pull into the driveway. It kinda startled me so I turned quickly. I was angry that it was three of Jim Martin's friends. I asked them what they wanted. I had hoped I'd never have to see them again. Matt came at me, raised his fist, and that's the last thing I remember until I woke up in the hospital with my brother and sister telling me I was okay."

Jacobs: "Now, Laura, you've seen the video and audio you accidentally took, correct?"

Laura: (Sighs heavily) "Yes, I've seen it just recently. My brother and sister didn't want me to see it until I was stronger. It shocked me as to what really happened."

Jacobs: "Okay, do you think you can handle seeing it now or would you like to leave the courtroom?"

Laura: "I'll be fine. I'll just sit right here, if that's okay."

Jacobs: "That's fine, Laura. Bailiff, will you please play the tape?"

The Bailiff went to the recorder and cued up the video to the large screen set up next to the Judge. As the video started, everyone smiled as they saw the beautiful flowers in Laura's yard. Their faces soon turned to horror as they saw Laura's view of Matt punching her. The three defendants just looked at each other. Their lawyer hadn't shown the tape to them, so they were as surprised as everyone else. It was apparent when Laura had fallen to the ground. The screen went black, but the audio was very clear. You could hear their nasty comments while they kicked her. Mrs. Walker's voice could be heard in the background. Then you heard the dogs and the men's attempt to get away from them. You could hear Derek screaming to get the dog off him. Then you heard Mrs. Walker's voice again, but, you couldn't make out what she said. Next, you heard Brutus whining and Mrs. Walker when she called 911. That was the end as Mrs. Walker closed the camera so she could call Elizabeth.

The Bailiff shut the video off. You could hear a pin drop in the courtroom. The horror that everyone just saw and heard was what Laura had lived.

Mr. Jacobs went up to Laura.

Jacobs: "Do you need a break?"

Laura: (Shaking her head) "No, I'm okay. I just want to get this over with."

Jacobs: "Let us know though if you do. Your Honor, I have no further questions."

Judge: (Kinda choking on his breathing) "Okay, Miss Parker, do you feel you can go on?"

Laura: "Yes, Your Honor, thank you. I'm fine."

Judge: "Mr. Bishop, do you have any questions?"

Bishop: "Uhh, Laura."

Laura: "Miss Parker, to you."

That brought a roll of laughter to the gallery, which brought a banging of the gavel by the Judge.

Bishop: "I'm sorry. Miss Parker, are you healing well?"

Laura: "Well, Mr. Bishop, I shouldn't have to answer a question like that now, should I?"

Bishop: "I have no further questions, Your Honor."

Judge: "Okay, Miss Parker, you may leave the stand. Do you need to take a recess?"

Laura: "No, thank you, Your Honor, I'm fine."

Judge: "Mr. Jacobs. Do you have any other witnesses?"

Jacobs: "No, Your Honor. The prosecution rests."

Judge: "Okay, this has been an emotional session, so I think we'll adjourn until 9 a.m. tomorrow. Court dismissed."

Chapter 52

Day three of the trial—June 30. The media had all different ideas of what kind of defense Edward Bishop will present. He really didn't have one. The tape and Laura's testimony yesterday were pretty powerful. The original defense, that they didn't do anything to Laura, just got blown out of the water. Unless they had doubles out there, there was no denying it was them on the tape. Jim Martin kept trying to deny that he had anything at all to do with the assault. The fact that he was named shot that notion to kingdom come.

8:45 a.m. The jury was seated, as was the Prosecutor. The defendants are brought in, unshackled, and seated. The gallery was filled. Elizabeth, Jeremiah, and Miss Peg were included in the galley but not Laura. After yesterday she couldn't handle coming in this morning. She'd be here for her Impact Statement but was building up the courage for that. The Judge okayed a videographer to have a closed-circuit TV set up at Laura's house. This way, she could watch the proceedings without exposing herself to the gawky stares she had to endure the day before. Beatrice

Walker was sitting with her, so she didn't have to deal with any more of this alone.

9 a.m. As usual, right on the dot, Judge Matthews entered the courtroom.

Bailiff: "All rise. The Honorable Brandon Matthews presiding. (Pause.) You may be seated."

The regular shuffling and chatter continued prompting the Judge to wield his gavel.

Judge: "Good morning, everyone. Mr. Bishop, are you ready to present your case?"

Bishop: "Well, yes and no, Your Honor."

Judge: "Which is it, Mr. Bishop? I'll not have you wasting this court's time."

Bishop: "Well, I have a character witness that is not present. We are trying to locate him. I beg the court's indulgence while we try to locate him."

Judge: "No, Mr. Bishop. My court starts at 9 a.m. I expect everyone to be present at that time. If they aren't, then we move on. Do you have anyone else to call? Obviously, that witness didn't want to testify after all. Move on."

Bishop: "That was about it, Your Honor. My clients have chosen not to testify, on their own behalf, at this time."

Judge: "Looks like we move on to the final arguments then the Witness Impact Statements. Mr. Bishop, you wanted to hold off on your opening argument. Are you prepared now?"

Bishop: "Actually, I waive the opening. I will go directly to the closing if it pleases the court."

Judge: "Mr. Jacobs, do you agree to let Mr. Bishop do his closing first?"

Jacobs: "Oh, by all means, Your Honor. I'm anxious to hear what he has to say."

Judge: "Okay, Mr. Bishop. The floor is yours."

Bishop got up, buttoned his jacket, looked around the courtroom, walked up to the jury box, and cleared his throat...stalling.

Bishop: "Ladies and Gentlemen, you've heard a lot of accusatory, and emotional testimony the last couple of days. I want you to put yourself in my clients' shoes for a minute. For example, James Martin is here by video feed because he is in prison for something he never believed he did wrong. He didn't kill David Parker; his father did. He simply chose not to say anything about it. His friends, Derek, Matt, and Andrew, agreed with him. They feel he shouldn't be sitting in jail just for that reason. They are all being charged with attempted murder. In James' case, conspiracy to attempted murder. All charges are way out of line. They merely wanted to go over and talk to Laura Parker to see if she would help to get their friend out of prison. As soon as they got to her house though she got angry...antagonizing them. She may be small but she has a mean mouth. They may have lost their tempers, but they didn't plan to kill her, as these charges suggest. They agree they shouldn't have assaulted her, but murder was never on their minds. Thank you."

Judge: "Hmm, is that all, Mr. Bishop?"

Bishop: "Yes, Your Honor, Thank You."

Judge: "Okay, Mr. Jacobs?"

Jacobs: "Hmm, murder was never on their minds, huh? Bailiff, would you replay the tape where we hear the defendants while they are attacking Miss Parker?"

Bailiff forwards the tape to the attack.

Matt: "Hey, Dogpatch. Jim Martin says hello."

Jacobs: "Please pause it.... Let's see...just mildly losing your temper, Matt?... With a fist breaking her jaw and knocking her unconscious? Please forward."

Matt: "We'll show you what happens when you mess with the wrong people."

Jacobs: "Pause.... You are the wrong people, all right.... Continue."

Derek: "You don't think we would forget how you took everything away from us, did you?"

Andrew: "We had it made until you showed up. You won't get away with what you've done"

Jacobs: "Pause the tape, please. Andrew, that's about the time you kicked her in the ribs, isn't it? Breaking three and making it very difficult for her to breathe. I think you need to be able to breathe to live. Continue tape."

Derek: "We'll make sure you never have the chance to do anything to anyone else."

Jacobs: "Stop the tape. That's about when you kicked her full force in the abdomen with your hiking boot, wasn't it, Derek? That statement sounded like more of a threat to me than anything. Laura Parker was already lying on the ground...unconscious...when you two just kept kicking her. She couldn't hear you. It was all your anger that your money tree died. And, Mr. Martin, you figured if she was out of the way, you could appeal your case. Without her as a witness, you just might win. Well, I have a shock for all of you. Yes, Laura Parker is small but strong and has a strong will to live. She survived the worst assault I have ever seen come across my desk."

"I would like to reiterate the size difference between these three men and Miss Parker. Matt...265 pounds, six-foot-three. Derek...289 pounds, six-foot-five. Andrew...230 pounds, six-foot-one. Laura Parker...107 pounds, five-foot-one at the time of the attack. She was also on the ground...limp as a rag doll, unable to defend herself at all."

"Thankfully the neighbor's dogs intervened. Now the one only weighs about 150 pounds, but, his body strength and fierce training were something none of you could match. I noticed you didn't stick around to fight him. From what I understand, the other dog, a two-hundred-pound rottweiler, lay down next to Laura so you couldn't get to her again. Those dogs showed the right kind of loyalty—protective. Your loyalty was fueled by the desire for money—apples to oranges—don't you agree? You three are cowards—following a leader who has no morals either."

"Laura Parker will go on with her life...not as it was before, but at least alive. Your comments though as you attacked her, tell me that, given the chance, you would have continued your attack. I'll never be able to comprehend how anyone can be so angry as to beat someone almost to death. I called you cowards, and I meant it. The one here with courage is Laura Parker. She refused to give up. Ladies and Gentlemen of the Jury, these men should be sent to the darkest recesses of prison. They certainly shouldn't be allowed to be out free to have the opportunity to do this to someone else...maybe succeeding in murdering someone the next time. Thank you."

With that, he sat down. Again the courtroom was dead silent as it was after hearing the tape the first time. There was a definite chill in the air.

Judge: "Mr. Jacobs, is Miss Parker available to make her Victim Impact Statement right now?"

Jacobs: "No, Your Honor. She just wasn't able to be physically in the courtroom this morning. She's still pretty fragile, so she remained at home. She did see the proceedings though on closed-circuit. I can have her here first thing this afternoon."

Judge: "Fine. Ladies and Gentlemen of the Jury. I will give you your instructions after Miss Parker's Victim Impact Statement. It will give you something to ponder over your lunch. We will adjourn until 1:30 p.m."

Gavel…. The Judge got up and left the courtroom.

Chapter 53

1:15 p.m. The jury, defendants, prosecutor, and gallery filled the courtroom.

At 1:30 p.m., Judge Matthews entered the courtroom.

The Bailiff called order. This time the courtroom was just quiet. Everyone anticipated Laura's statement. Everyone felt there was something missing. They knew there had been at least five weeks between the attack, the men's arrest, and the trial. Something dramatic had to have gone on that hadn't come to light yet.

Judge: "Mr. Jacobs, is Miss Parker here to make her Victim Impact Statement?"

Jacobs: "Yes, Your Honor. I was just waiting until you were present before calling her in. She is understandably nervous. She was worried about being surrounded by the media. I'll have her come in now."

He turned, and Jeremiah left the room to get Laura. They were flanked by two Kester police officers for

Laura's protection. They walked Laura to the podium, then the officers left. Jeremiah took his seat next to Elizabeth after giving her hand a squeeze for encouragement.

As anticipated, the courtroom buzz started almost immediately. Laura was wearing a mask today though. Her appearance upset *her* enough. She didn't want any comments from the gallery. The Judge pounded his gavel several times to quiet the room. He could see, like the last time that Laura stood at that podium, that she was nervous and close to tears. He whispered something to the Bailiff.

The Bailiff whispered to Laura, "Just in case," and smiled as he handed her a box of tissues.

Laura gave him a look of gratitude.

Judge: "Miss Parker, are you able to make your statement here today or do you need more time?"

Laura: (Smiling with her eyes) "Thank you for your consideration, Your Honor, but I need to do this now. I've been working on what to say, so I need to get it out."

Judge: "Okay, Miss Parker. But if you need to stop or take a break you just let me know, all right?"

Laura: "Yes, Your Honor."

"Ladies and Gentlemen of the Jury, I stand here in front of you only by the Grace of God. I am a firm believer in the Power of Prayer. My sister told me that during both of my surgeries, a prayer group from St. Matthew's Catholic Church kinda tag-teamed each other so there would be a group there praying for me all the time. It must have been true, like I believed, because here I stand...still shaky but standing just the same."

"After my attack, I lost about three weeks of my life. My injuries were such that the doctors felt I wouldn't be able to endure the pain or the realization of what I would eventually have to live with. For that reason they kept me sedated."

"I will start at the beginning. Please be patient with me because I still have trouble speaking and accepting what has happened to me. As my grandmother used to say when she had a long story to tell, 'This will take a minute.' I'm sure most of you know what that means."

"When Matt Roman hit me, he changed my appearance forever. I have a lot of surgeries to endure yet before my jaw is entirely back to the way a jaw should sit. I joked with the surgeon that I've never been beautiful…maybe he can do that for me since he'll be working on it anyway. Right now though I'm just looking forward to the day I can bite into solid food and chew it. Everything I eat now comes out of the blender. Some day I'll again have a stable jaw and teeth but not for a while."

"The surgery to just put my jaw somewhat back together, took over fourteen hours. Just imagine standing that long, concentrating on slivers of bone, and trying to figure out where the other piece of that bone could be. That was what the surgeons that worked on me dealt with. That is dedication. I don't know about you, but the thought makes my feet and back hurt. From what I see and feel though they did a pretty good job. Next time you pick up a toothpick, think about it. They put a bunch of bones like that together and gave me my jaw back."

"That was—well—the happy surgery. It was after three weeks that they had to wait to do this surgery because my body was still reeling from the first surgery.

I was still struggling with my breathing and blood pressure. Another X-ray showed I had three broken ribs. Thankfully they had the solution. They bound my chest to stabilize my ribs...problem was solved."

"When the ambulance got me to the hospital that Saturday, the EMTs told the doctors that my abdomen was swelling and there was some vaginal bleeding. The X-ray they took showed a fluid build-up, but they didn't know where it was coming from. I was rushed into surgery within an hour of arriving at the ER. That was the only way to see where the fluid buildup was."

"Elizabeth, could I have my bottle of water?"

Elizabeth handed it to her. It already had a straw to make it easy for her to drink.

Laura: "I'm sorry, Your Honor, all of a sudden, I felt very parched."

Judge: "Miss Parker, do you need a break? Take your time."

Laura: "No, just a drink, thank you. I can continue. I'm sorry this is so long."

Judge: "This is your statement to let everyone know how this attack affects you. Continue when you can and take as much time as you need."

Laura: "Thank you, Your Honor. Okay, the surgery I had right after being admitted to the ER took five hours. The doctors estimated three but there was more to do than they thought. My brother, Jeremiah, was in school in Chicago when my sister called him to tell him what happened. He had a four- to five-hour drive to get here and arrived just before I got out of surgery. Mrs. Walker, our neighbor, came to sit with my sister, Elizabeth, before Jeremiah got there so she wouldn't be alone. Sheriff Stone, I was told, was there most of the time, too."

"When the surgery was over, the news wasn't good. The doctors knew that they would have to remove my spleen. More often than not, that happens from an abdominal injury. That wasn't the bad part. (Laura had to stop for a few seconds; the tears started to flow.) I'm sorry, this is tough for me. When I was kicked, by Derek, the kick was so forceful that it bruised my kidney and bladder. (Sigh.) The horrible part was my female organs had been shredded. The doctors worked for hours to try to repair them, but were unsuccessful. They had to make the decision to remove everything."

"When I woke up three weeks later, everyone danced around telling me that until I forced them to tell me. This is especially devastating for many reasons.

"My dad was killed when I was eighteen. The twins were eleven. My mom died when I was twenty-one, and the twins, fourteen. That's when I gained full guardianship of them. My parents had specific plans for all of us. The main one was that we would go to college and attain our dreams. When Mom died, I became the primary breadwinner of the family. Up to my attack I actually worked at three jobs to make sure my bother and sister got the education they needed to pursue their careers. I never saw anything else...just get the kids through school."

"I'm thirty-one years old. I figured I could go back to school once they were out.... Get married and have a family. I don't see the last two things happening. I'm going to tell the court something that no one knows. I just hope the media doesn't manage to mock me for it. I'm a staunch Catholic. I don't believe in premarital relations. I'll let you fill in the blanks. I've never dated.

I didn't have time. Now...because...because...these men were angry for losing their money source, and took it out on me, I may never know the joy so many of you that are married take for granted. And...I'll never be a mom."

"This is what these men took from me. I know for a fact, none of them are celibate. Change that situation for them. Take from them what they took from me. They should not be allowed the freedom to do as they wish any longer."

"There is a baby in heaven that was supposed to be mine. It will never know what a great mom I would have been. When Mr. Bishop questioned me, the only thing he could ask was how was I healing. I will never heal from this kind of hurt."

"The one thing I ask, Your Honor, is that you find a way that they aren't in jail together...if they go to jail. They don't deserve to continue their friendship; it would be dangerous if they were together."

"Thank you for listening to this lengthy statement but you needed to know it all."

With that, Laura, crying, sat down between Jeremiah and Elizabeth. She looked at the jury and saw at least one woman had been crying. She got to them as she had hoped. The room was silent.

Even the Judge was stunned by her statement. He didn't see that coming. He knew now that he needed to be careful in giving the jury their instructions.

Judge: "Mr. Jacobs, is there anyone else that you feel needs to speak at this time?"

Jacobs: "No, Your Honor. I think Miss Parker said it all."

Judge: "Very well. Ladies and Gentlemen of the Jury. You have heard all the evidence in this case. I'll give you your instructions then you will retire to the jury room. Take as long as you need to render a verdict in this case."

"You have two primary duties as jurors. The first one is to decide what the facts are from the evidence that you saw and heard here in court. Choosing what the facts are is your job, not mine, and nothing I have said or done during this trial was meant to influence your decision about the facts in any way."

"Your second job is to take the law I give you, apply it to the facts, and decide if the government has proved the defendants guilty beyond a reasonable doubt."

"You are bound by the oath you took at the beginning of the trial to follow the instructions that I give you, even if you personally disagree with one or more of them."

"As you know, the defendants have pleaded not guilty to the crimes charged in the indictment. The indictment is not any evidence at all of guilt. It is just the formal way that the government tells the defendant what crimes he is accused of committing. It does not even raise any suspicion of guilt."

"No defendant has any obligation to present any evidence at all or to prove to you in any way that he is innocent. It is up to the government to prove that he is guilty."

"If you are convinced that the government, through the evidence, has proved the defendants guilty beyond a reasonable doubt, then the proper verdict is 'guilty.' If you are not convinced, a 'not guilty' verdict must be returned."

"You must make your decision based only on the evidence that you saw and heard here in court. Do not let rumors, suspicions, or anything else that you may have seen or heard outside of court influence your decision in any way."

"It would be best if you used your common sense in weighing the evidence. Consider it in light of your everyday experience with people and events, and give it whatever weight you believe it deserves. If your experience tells you that certain evidence reasonably leads to a conclusion, you are free to reach that conclusion."

"Part of your job as jurors is to decide how believable each witness was. This is your job, not mine. It is up to you to determine whether a witness's testimony was credible, and how much weight you think it deserves."

"Ask yourself if the witness was able to clearly see or hear the events."

"Ask yourself how good the witness's memory seemed to be.

"Ask yourself if there was anything else that may have interfered with the witnesses' ability to perceive or remember the events."

"Ask yourself how the witness looked and acted while testifying."

"Ask yourself if the witness had any relationship to either side of the case."

"Finally, ask yourself how believable the witness's testimony was in light of all the other evidence."

"A conspiracy is a kind of criminal partnership. For you to find the defendant guilty of the conspiracy charge, the government must prove both of the following essential ingredients (or 'elements') beyond a reasonable doubt:

"First, that two or more persons conspired, or agreed, to commit the crime;

"Second, that the defendant knowingly and voluntarily joined the conspiracy intending to help advance or achieve its goal."

"You must be convinced that the government has proved both of these things beyond a reasonable doubt to find the defendant guilty of the conspiracy charge."

"The defendants have been charged with two crimes. The number of charges is no evidence of guilt, and this should not influence your decision in any way. It is your duty to separately consider the evidence that relates to each charge, and to return a separate verdict for each one."

"The defendant has an absolute right not to testify. The fact that the defendants did not testify cannot be considered by you in any way or even discussed in your deliberations."

"I remind you that it is up to the government to prove the defendant guilty beyond a reasonable doubt. It is not up to the defendant to prove that he is innocent."

"The first thing you should do in the jury room is choose someone to be your foreperson. This person will help guide your discussions and speak for you here in court."

"Once you start deliberating, do not talk to the jury officer, me or anyone else about the case. We must communicate in writing. Write down your message, sign it, and give it to the jury officer. He will give it to me, and I will respond as soon as I can."

"These are your preliminary instructions. I'll release you now for you to go to lunch and then begin your deliberations. Court will be adjourned until the jury has reached their verdict."

It was 3:30 p.m. Laura had taken nearly two hours to give her statement. She did have to take her time. It was still very difficult for her to talk. She had been determined though to tell it all.

The Bailiffs and Kester Police got Laura and the twins out of the courthouse in record time. They were out of there before people realized they were gone.

Miss Peg, on the other hand, just sat in her seat in the courtroom. Laura had disclosed things that she didn't even know. The fact that Laura had never dated never crossed her mind. Laura had been her employee, so she had never delved into her personal life that deeply. She knew she cleaned houses after she left her house, but she didn't know this took up her entire life. It made her very sad that she never paid attention more to Laura. She had considered her a friend. A friend should know things like that...but she didn't.

Mostly she was overwhelmed by what James and his friends had done to her. Because of them she would never have a baby. She was the most gentle and generous person she knew. Something Patrick started more than ten years ago came down to this. She just wished there was something more she could do to help. Once all this was over she would reach out to the Parker children. It hurt her heart that her family has done so much harm to this family...a family that actually had taken care of her family. Somehow she had to make at least some of this right.

Chapter 54

A little after 4:15 p.m., the Parkers pulled into the drive with their security in tow. Now that Laura had made such an emotionally damning statement, the Prosecutor didn't want her left unprotected. He remembers how nasty it got for her after Jim Martin's trial. Granted, it was primarily the other three defendants who had spurred the uproar, but they had friends, too, that might try something. This case was so different. Laura had been directly impacted. The Prosecutor knew the results of her emergency surgery. It wasn't his place though to bring it up during the trial. He figured she would find a way. It definitely was something the jury needed to know. It hit them hard when they heard her tell her story. He doubted any of them would be walking free after that.

Jeremiah cooked them all a nice dinner, but no one was very hungry. Pork chops out of a blender are really not that appealing. Jeremiah encouraged Laura to eat something though. She had lost a lot of weight in the hospital. She didn't weigh a hundred pounds. She couldn't afford to lose any more weight.

At 7 p.m., the phone rang. It was Mr. Jacobs. The jury had some questions for the Judge before they rendered their verdict. They just wanted to get it all right. As of ten minutes ago, they had their verdict. They were all due back in court at 7:30 p.m. They had to hurry. Their security detail wasted no time getting them there. At 7:18 p.m., they pulled up to the courthouse. Word had gotten out that the verdict was in, so every reporter around the area who had been following the case was there. The officers closed in close so the Parkers could get into the courtroom.

7:30 p.m., Judge Matthews walked to the bench.

Bailiff: "All rise. The Honorable Brandon Matthews presiding. You may be seated."

Judge: "Mr. Jacobs, I understand the jury has reached its verdict."

Jacobs: "Yes, they have, Your Honor."

Judge: "Bailiffs, will you bring in the defendants?"

The defendants were brought in—shackled. The shackles were left on for everyone's protection this time. They sat down.

Judge: "Bailiff, will you bring in the jury?"

The courtroom was church quiet as the jurors shuffled their way to their seats. They didn't look up or at anyone.

Judge: "I expect complete quiet while the jury foreman reads the verdicts. One outburst and I will have the bailiffs clear the courtroom. If that is clear we will proceed."

"Mr. Foreman, I understand you have reached a verdict."

Jury Foreman: (Standing) "We have, Your Honor."

Judge: "Please hand it to the Clerk."

The Clerk took the folded paper from the Foreman and brought it to the Judge. The Judge read the entire paper and then handed it back to the Clerk who took it back to the jury foreman.

Judge: "Will the defendants rise? That includes you, too, Mr. Martin."

"We will take one charge at a time. On the First Count, Assault, how do you find the defendant, Matthew Roman?"

Foreman: "We find the defendant: Guilty."

Judge: "On the First Count, Assault, how do you find the defendant, Derek Sanders?"

Foreman: "We find the defendant: Guilty."

Judge: "On the First Count—Assault, how do you find the defendant: Andrew Cassidy?"

Foreman: "We find the defendant: Guilty."

Judge: "On the First Count—Conspiracy to Commit Assault, how do you find the defendant, James Martin?"

Foreman: "We find the defendant: Guilty."

Judge: "On the Second Count—Second Degree Attempted Murder, how do you find the defendant, Matthew Roman?"

Foreman: "We find the defendant: Guilty."

Judge: "On the Second Count—Second Degree Attempted Murder, how do you find the defendant, Derek Sanders?"

Foreman: "We find the defendant: Guilty."

Judge: "On the Second Count—Second Degree Attempted Murder, how do you find the defendant, Andrew Cassidy?"

Foreman: "We find the defendant: Guilty."

Judge: "On the Second Count—Conspiracy to Second Degree Attempted Murder, how do you find the defendant, James Martin?"

Foreman: "We find the defendant: Guilty."

The courtroom erupted in both cheers and angry "Nos." The Bailiffs quickly removed the angry people from the gallery. The Judge had to keep banging his gavel to quiet everyone down. The Parkers just held on to one another. Miss Peg stood up with tears in her eyes and hugged Laura for a very long time. It took several minutes to quiet the courtroom down. But when it was quiet, the Judge took over.

Judge: "Ladies and Gentlemen of the Jury, I thank you for your service in this matter. I know it was a difficult case to judge. You have seen and heard things you hope you'll never see or hear again. The court will reconvene tomorrow, July 1st, when I will render my decisions as to sentences for all four defendants."

"Miss Parker, I am truly sorry that you have gone through all you have these last months. My hopes for you are that you are able to attain some of your wishes for your future. Court dismissed."

The Judge left the bench, and the courtroom emptied in minutes. Laura, Elizabeth, and Jeremiah sat there for a few minutes until it was comfortable for them to leave. Sheriff Stone and two of his deputies came up to them.

Sheriff Stone: "Laura, my deputies, and I will escort you to the car so you don't get swamped by reporters."

Laura: "Actually, Sheriff, I would like to make a short statement. Maybe if I do and answer a couple of questions, they'll back off for a while. The only thing I ask is don't let anyone close enough to pull off my mask. I don't want that picture all over the media."

Sheriff: "That may be a good idea. I'll have Kester PD officers help keep them away. Are you ready to go?"

Laura: "I would also like to have a couple of officers protecting Miss Peg. There were some nasty things said to her in court. I want to make sure she's safe, too. We can go if you have all of this under control."

Sheriff: "Definitely."

Between County and City there were six officers around Laura and the twins. There were two officers protecting Miss Peg. They stopped at the top of the courthouse steps. Reporters pressed in with their phones and microphones, as close as the officers would allow. Laura took a step forward and raised her hand for quiet.

Laura: "Hi, Everyone. Your interest in this has really surprised me. I saw a recording of the news report the night I was attacked. The emphasis that night was the three rich men who had been arrested. What they had done to me kinda took a back seat. After tonight's verdict, you can see privilege is not a get-out-of-jail-free card. What those men did had consequences—some I will live with for the rest of my life. After tomorrow we'll see their consequences. I'll take a couple of questions."

First Reporter: "Are you going to sue for damages from these four men?"

Laura: "One step at a time. I just wanted this part over. There is time to proceed."

Second Reporter: "Laura, where do you go from here?"

Laura: "Right now, home knowing I'm safe and alive and that, hopefully, these men will never have the opportunity to take their anger out on anyone else. Thank you, everyone. I want to get some needed rest."

With that, the officers closed the path so they all could get to their cars. Laura stopped to give Miss Peg one last long hug. You could hear the cameras go off. That picture would probably go out with some snarky comment along with it. "Victim Hugs Attacker's Mother."

Chapter 55

Day five of the trial.

9 a.m., Judge Matthews took the bench.

The Bailiff called order to the court.

The gallery was already full. Laura, Elizabeth, and Jeremiah were in the first row. Miss Peg was right behind them. Bailiffs brought in the defendants. There were extra bailiffs behind the defendants as well as extra security around the courtroom and outside. Most of the people in the gallery were family and friends of the defendants with a few reporters. Judge Matthews didn't want any trouble today when he imposed sentences on all the defendants.

The Judge looked out into the courtroom. All was quiet. The defendants had the look of defiance on their · faces. Jim Martin just looked angry. The Judge looked at Laura and felt a pang of hurt at what she had had to endure at the hands of these four angry men.

Judge: "I thought long and hard as to what my decision on the sentences should be for these defendants. Their heinous disregard for another person's life is beyond belief. From what I've been told, the three defendants here in the courtroom had very good jobs. Considering they're all single their paychecks should have been sufficient to afford them an excellent lifestyle. The obvious problem here though is that they were angry that they had to spend their own money on entertainment. When James Martin was around, he seemed to have money to burn, even after his father died. When he was held accountable for his deception over the years about David Parker's death, everyone's party money stopped."

"James Martin was still angry. He blamed the Parkers for his father dying from guilt over killing their father. Something was definitely backward. Mr. Jacobs called that *misplaced anger* during Mr. Martin's original trial. Fast forward to now. Mr. Martin's anger had been passed to his lifelong friends. They thought as Mr. Martin did: If Laura were not around, he might be able to talk his way out of prison...thus everyone would have the free money again."

Bishop: (Jumps up) "Your Honor!!"

Judge: "Sit down, Mr. Bishop. The defendants are going to hear what I have to say and understand why I will impose the sentences I am about to give them."

Bishop sat down but just shook his head. He was more upset about the Judge's comments than his clients were.

Judge: "As I was saying before being interrupted by defendants' counsel, there will be no more free money for any of the defendants. The only money they'll see is what their families send to the commissaries at their facilities."

"The sentences I am about to impose will be served concurrently. That means together. So, the sentence for Assault and the sentence for the Second Degree Attempted Murder will be served together. Will the defendants rise? That includes you, too, Mr. Martin. Will the guard there see to it that he is standing?"

"First, Mr. Martin, for your sentence for Conspiracy to Assault, there will be three years added to the sentence you are now serving. Along with that, on the Second Count of Conspiracy to Attempted Murder, I am adding ten to forty years to your sentence. You will be eligible for parole now in twenty-eight years. This includes the time you are currently serving."

James: (Screaming) "That isn't fair. I never touched that bitch. She had it coming, though!"

Judge: "Guard, quiet the prisoner down. Mr. Martin, if you aren't silent, I will see to it that you are sent back to solitary instead of your cell block. Is that understood?"

Bishop: "Jim, answer him."

James: "Yes, Your Honor."

Judge: "Fine. Since all three of you, Matthew Roman, Derek Sanders, and Andrew Cassidy, all participated in the attack of Laura Parker, the sentences will all be the same."

"For the Assault of Laura Parker, I sentence you, Matthew Roman, Derek Sanders, and Andrew Cassidy, to three to ten years in prison."

"For the Second Degree of Attempted Murder of Laura Parker, I sentence you, Matthew Roman, Derek

Sanders, and Andrew Cassidy, to ten to eighty years in prison."

"You will be eligible for parole in ten years, no sooner. Even though the assault sentence is shorter."

"I am going to honor the request of the victim in this case. My recommendation to the Department of Corrections is that you all serve your sentences in different facilities. Say goodbye to your friends, fellas. This will likely be the last you will see of them."

Bailiffs, take the defendants back to their cells to wait to be transferred. This court is adjourned."

The Judge stopped and looked directly at Laura and smiled. He hoped he brought her some peace.

The reporters who had been able to squeeze into the courtroom went rushing out. You could hear them shouting the Judge's sentences to everyone in earshot.

The Roman, Sanders, and Cassidy families just stood there in shocked silence. All their money and influence couldn't keep their sons out of prison, for what could amount to the rest of their lives. Their hopes of passing their businesses on to their sons had been dashed. The one thing that none of them even considered was what Laura had gone through. A decent person would have at least apologized. Not them though. They just gave Laura some very angry looks.

Miss Peg though was an altogether different kind of person. She couldn't seem to apologize enough. She had compassion for Laura more than all those other parents combined. Laura turned to her and said, "I'm sorry." She knew how heartbroken Miss Peg was about both Patrick and James' actions. Miss Peg had gotten caught up in the middle even though she wasn't party to any of the deceptions. Miss Peg just shook her head "no" to show it wasn't something Laura should be sorry about. She again folded her into her arms. They were both crying by this time.

They all walked out together surrounded by their security. The Prosecutor told them to go home. He would make a statement to the press. Laura was more than happy to oblige.

Once the Parkers were whisked out past the reporters, Mr. Jacobs faced the reporters.

Jacobs: "Ladies and Gentlemen. Even though this trial only took five days to complete, the case started about two years ago when James Martin was imprisoned for obstruction and knowledge after the fact. As he feels now and how he felt then was he did nothing wrong. Unfortunately, he has a very persuasive personality. He pulled three men into his circle of anger. Today was the culmination of their poor decisions. The victim, Laura Parker though can now move on and heal. Make smart decisions, people. You see what happens when you don't."

When Laura got home she sat down, put her feet up, and her head back, removed her mask, and just started to cry. All the bad stuff that had been done to her, and said to and about her, was over. She could now begin to really heal.

Chapter 56

As planned, Jeremiah left for France on July 9. He didn't want to leave his sisters, but at least he knew now they were safe. Laura did as she promised and practically kicked his butt all the way to the airport. His first couple weeks there would be hectic but pleasant at the same time. His fiancée, Georgette, was going to France with him. She was using a couple of weeks of this year's vacation to see as much of France as possible with Jeremiah when he wasn't in school. She was going to see if she could sit in on a couple of classes. You never know. Besides, they decided to use this as an early honeymoon. They wouldn't have the money after they got married to make this kind of trip.

Along with his fellowship at the Culinary School, Jeremiah was given a small flat not too far from the school. His airfare was even covered. They only had to pay for Georgette's airfare and their food. You can't get a cheaper trip to France than that.

Laura kinda frowned at them being together in France but didn't say too much. They were adults, after all. She wasn't going to impose her ideals on anyone else. She, better than anyone else, learned not to hold on to something so hard that you lose things around it. They had the right to enjoy as much time together as they could muster.

He'd be back just in time for Elizabeth's wedding in January. She was getting married on the 22nd, and he'd walk her down the aisle. It would be a beautiful day.

Chapter 57

Life for the Parkers quieted down within weeks of the trial. As with most things like this, people tire of all the hoopla. Laura could finally just go to the store and not be hounded. What a relief.

Laura's first reconstructive surgery was the week after Jeremiah left for France. This was the one that would align her bottom gums with her top teeth. She'd be out for a while during this one. Miss Peg sat with Elizabeth for the four hours the doctors worked on Laura. She'd be bruised, swollen, and sore afterward. The doctors hadn't decided yet what to do about the teeth she had lost. She'd probably just be able to wear a denture. At first, they considered implants since they would have her gums open but eventually decided against it. The denture would give her more support to her jaw. It had been so shattered that it would never be very stable. An implant could tear her gums if she tried to eat something hard. The denture could be fitted as soon as the swelling went down, so it would line up with her upper teeth.

Laura's strength showed through again. Even with a bruised and swollen jaw she attempted to smile when she woke up. She was healing inside and out.

When the dressing and packing were removed two weeks after the surgery she ran her tongue over her new gums. That was when her smile got the biggest.

Laura: "Doctor, the gum feels pretty smooth considering you cut it up pretty good. What's next?"

Surgeon: "I want the swelling to go down completely, then we'll fit you for a denture. Give it until about September though. We want it to be a gum we can form a denture on. There is good news though. If you want, you can start on soft foods. Instead of pureed, just mushed...macaroni and cheese, canned tuna...you really don't have to chew. Something of that nature where you need to move your jaw up and down. Here also is a sheet of exercises to strengthen the joint and the muscles. It will be tight so don't push the exercises to the point of pain. Start slow."

Laura: "Thank you, Doctor. I'll set an appointment for September."

On August 6, Elizabeth sat for State Boards for her PA Certification. She was a wreck. She had to go to Springfield to take them, which was a couple of hours away. Her fiancé, Carl, decided to spend the day with Laura. Carl had already passed his boards to be a pharmacist, so he knew the butterflies bouncing around in Elizabeth's belly right now. He wanted her to be completely focused, so that's why he was staying with Laura. Both Elizabeth and Jeremiah had hovered over Laura since the attack. He didn't want either one of them to worry that Laura would be left alone. Jeremiah called Carl at about 4 a.m. to make sure he was with Laura. Elizabeth called him when she got to Springfield. He was with Laura when Elizabeth called. She took the phone from him.

Laura: "Now look. I am fine. Carl is here. You just pay attention to your test, not me. I couldn't be any safer or better cared for right now. I'm praying for you. You'll do fine."

She hung up the phone and just sat there and laughed with Carl.

For the next week, everyone walked on eggshells. Elizabeth was pretty sure she had done well, but you never know. She had second guessed herself a couple of times. She hoped she ultimately made the right decisions.

On August 12, she got the results. SHE PASSED!! 98.2 percent correct. She'd have no way of knowing which ones she got wrong, but it didn't matter at this point. She was now a PA-C (Physician's Assistant-Certified). The first thing she did was call Jeremiah. It's a twin thing, apparently. After that, she called Carl. He was working so that call had to be short. It was time to celebrate. She didn't want to wait for Jeremiah to get home though. They'd just video chat with him over dinner. This party would include Laura, Elizabeth, Carl, Georgette, and Miss Peg. Miss Peg had been very helpful and supportive of Elizabeth. She had become like a second mother to the Parker children, and they now included her in everything.

Chapter 58

Speaking of Miss Peg, she went to see James after the sentencing. It was a good thing they weren't within reach of each other. James was still so angry that she had called the police resulting in his first trial and incarceration to start with. Another reason was that she sided with the Prosecutor about Laura's assault. She was there for less than ten minutes. He was still screaming at her when she walked out the door. His temper was still his undoing. He had a black eye and swollen cheek. There was someone there with better reach and a quicker temper. It's doubtful that this would be his last beating. He was in a facility close enough for Miss Peg to visit him but she doubted she ever would again.

The other three men weren't that lucky. Matt Roman was in Wyoming, Andrew Cassidy was in Colorado, and Derek Sanders was in New Mexico. They weren't fairing much better than James. Inmates have a way of finding out why a person is in prison.

The prisoners in Wyoming found out directly from Matt why he was there. No matter the reason someone is in prison, not too many like an abuser. That's what they considered Matt. It was a minimum security facility, so at least a couple of men had internet access. One of them looked up Laura's assault. All the time, the fact that Matt was parading around, angry that he was there but proud of what he had done, didn't sit well with a couple other inmates. If they could have gotten away with it, they would have done to him what he had done to Laura. He was lucky the guards were there to pull the four men off of him. They spent a couple of days in solitary, but he spent ten days in the infirmary, then a day in solitary. The guards figured he had started the fight.

The inmates at the other two facilities weren't any more forgiving. The inmates in Colorado figured they'd keep Andrew from eating for a while until he lost enough weight. They figured that it would only take one of them to give him some of his own medicine. When he got to the facility, he still weighed close to 230 pounds. He was bigger than some of the inmates. They had seen the pictures of Laura, too. They didn't like his cocky attitude. Let him get really hungry, then they'd let him have it. They were just biding their time.

Now, New Mexico was a little tougher facility. There were a lot of locals. It was still minimum security, but the men were sneakier. Some of these men were both drug and human smugglers who had finally gotten caught. They were good at hiding things—like shivs. One of them talked to his attorney and actually got a copy of Laura's Impact Statement. Now these men weren't violent offenders for the most part. Most of them had wives and children. When they found out about Laura, they were just plain—well—pissed. These were family men who believed in family. The crimes they committed were to be able to support their families. You don't lay your hands on a woman. In their eyes, that was a mortal sin. Derek paid for that. They didn't plan on killing him...just make him hurt real bad. Shivs and three men surrounded him in the yard one beautiful day. By the time they were done, he was sliced on every part of his body. Only his face was saved. Again, these men went to solitary confinement, but Derek hurt really bad. Most of the cuts got infected, so he was laid up for a couple of months.

The only reason for this was "Karma Is a Bitch."

Chapter 59

By the end of September, Laura had her dentures. She wasn't shy about smiling now. Next week would be her final plastic surgery to remove any scarring on her cheek.

After her last plastic surgery, she sat in the doctor's office. He was taking off the dressings and smiling. He handed Laura the mirror. She couldn't believe how well all the scars had disappeared.

Doctor: "Well, I did what I promised."

Laura: "What was that?"

Doctor: "I made you beautiful."

Laura started to cry. She never considered herself beautiful. Even now she looked just like she did before the attack. The doctor called her beautiful though. That made her feel beautiful.

The planning for Elizabeth's wedding was in full swing. Everything would be perfect. She and Georgette, and a couple of friends who would be bridesmaids, had all gotten their gowns. Food, entertainment, flowers, church, and venue were all on track. Now they just have to wait for the day to arrive. Carl and Elizabeth were both just giddy. After today's visit with the doctor Laura would have what she wanted, too. She no longer had to wear a mask, so the wedding pictures would be perfect.

October brought the crispness in the air that Midwesterners look forward to. Pumpkins and cornstalks graced all porches. Children were excited to put on the Halloween costumes and to go trick-or-treating.

November and December were lonely for Laura and Elizabeth because Jeremiah wasn't there to celebrate the holidays with them. He sent home some wonderful chocolates from an exclusive shop in Paris. Most men can't shop for a woman, but Jeremiah was different. He found a couple of lovely blouses and slacks from a French boutique for a Christmas gift for Laura. He found some delicate lace for Elizabeth for her wedding veil. These wonderful gifts didn't make up for him not being home. He'd be home in two weeks though. Those two weeks couldn't go by fast enough.

Chapter 60

As anticipated, the wedding was perfect. Laura sat in the first pew in the church in place of her parents. Sitting next to her though was an eight-by-ten picture of Sharon and David. Elizabeth was a beautiful bride. She was just glowing. If Carl had smiled any bigger, he would never have had been able to stop. Jeremiah walked Elizabeth down the aisle and then stood next to Carl as his best man. When he gets married, Carl will stand up for him. These four young people were very close. They were also all very protective of Laura.

Unlike Jeremiah and Georgette, Elizabeth and Carl waited to take their honeymoon. They took a week and went to New York. Elizabeth was excited to get a street cart hot dog. Carl looked forward to an authentic piece of New York cheesecake. They both wanted a pastrami sandwich from one of the famous delis. They went to a Broadway play and walked through Central Park. For a change they could think of just themselves.

Georgette was also a beautiful bride when she and Jeremiah got married in March. Again Laura sat in the same pew with their parents' picture beside her. This time the places for the twins were reversed. It dawned on Laura that the house would be empty except for her. That made her a little sad but happy at the same time. She had done it! The twins were secure in their careers and now both had joined with their life mates. David and Sharon would have been very proud to see this. Not only did the twins reach their goal—they fulfilled their parents' dream for them. Laura was on cloud nine.

Chapter 61

Right after Memorial Day, Miss Peg wanted to start planning for a big 4th of July party at her house. It was going to include anyone from town who cared to attend. There was plenty of room to accommodate a lot of people. It would take a lot of coordinating to pull this all off. Food. Games. Entertainment. Fireworks. Laura spent a lot of time before Memorial Day at the Martin Estate to work with Benjamin to start pulling this all together. It was going to be a great party. The announcement for it would be a full-page ad in the *News-Sentinel*. Robert Baker, the owner of the *Sentinel* and father of Trinity Baker, might not like Miss Peg but he couldn't ignore the revenue the full-page ad and all the subsequent ads it would generate.

On Wednesday, June 1st, Laura went out to the Martins to meet with Miss Peg and the ad exec from the *Sentinel*. Putting the ad together would take time.

She walked into the kitchen and met all the ladies she used to work side-by-side with. She noticed Miss Peg's food was still on her tray. It was almost 9 a.m. She was usually down for breakfast by 8 a.m.

Laura: "Why hasn't Miss Peg eaten yet?"

Joanne: "She just hasn't come downstairs yet. I'm keeping it warm."

Laura: "Has she been getting up this late?"

Joanne: "She did a couple of days last week. She told us she was just overly tired."

Laura: "Well, the guy from the paper is due here at ten so I'll go get her and remind her."

Laura was humming and thinking about all she wanted in the ad, even though she knew most of it wouldn't fit. She knocked on Miss Peg's door. Hmm, she must still be asleep. She quietly walked in and went to the bed to wake her....She wasn't sleeping. She had a book in her hand that she had been reading. The bedside light was on. Laura could tell by the pallor on Miss Peg's face that she had been dead for a while. She just stood there for a minute. The tears came fast and full force. This remarkable woman was gone. It appeared she had fallen asleep reading and passed in her sleep. She did have a very peaceful look on her face.

She walked out and gently closed the door. Telling everyone would be the hardest thing she's had to do in a long time. She walked to Benjamin's office, but he wasn't there. She found everyone in the kitchen, gathered like every morning as they waited for Miss Peg's daily instructions. Laura was relieved she didn't have to call anyone in special to give them the sad news.

Laura: "Hey, everyone. Quiet for a minute, okay? Whew...this is tough. I'll just say it. Miss Peg passed away sometime in the middle of the night. I knew something was wrong as soon as I walked into her room. She looks so peaceful. I'm thankful this is how God chose to take her."

Everyone at this point was crying harder than Laura had ever seen. Bethany, Miss Peg's personal maid, was shaking so badly she needed to sit down. The look on Charles' face was utter disbelief. Laura let everyone just cry for a few minutes before she went on with what needed to be done.

Laura: "This is not something any of us even remotely could imagine right now, but there are things that have to be done. I need to call the sheriff and have him come out with the coroner. He has to come out because she died at home. When they leave, I'll call McCullough's. Benjamin, I think you should contact Mr. Lancaster and tell him. I know there are things he has to do right away according to her will."

"This is the worst day any of us can imagine, but now we must act like Miss Peg is directing us. Oh, man, the guy from the newspaper is here. I'm just going to tell him we can't meet with him today. I don't want him blabbing this to the press yet."

"Joanne, to keep your head and heart occupied, how about you start planning the meal after the funeral, okay?"

Joanne: "Yes, uh, yes. Miss Peg had specific things she wanted. I have the list here. I'll get everyone working on the food and the house. Oh my. How will we all get through this?"

Laura: "Miss Peg trained us all, and we all know her likes, dislikes, and just how she would want things done. Let's all work like she is standing over our shoulders and telling us how she wants it. Is everyone okay with that? We'll all have a rough time over the next couple of weeks. We have each other to lean on though. No one has to go through this alone. Let's lean on each other like only we know how to do. If you have to cry—go ahead. No one will fault you for it. At the same time though let's honor Miss Peg by doing everything perfectly. I need to go head off this ad guy. Please go to work, everyone."

Laura explained to the ad exec that Miss Peg wasn't up to meeting with him today, and she would call him if the situation changed. He seemed satisfied with that and left.

One thing was out of the way. Now to call Sheriff Stone.

The reporters in this town could smell when something was up. Either that or someone saw the Sheriff and the coroner at the Martin Estate. The Sheriff saw a news van start up the drive. He hurried and cut them off without giving them any information. It would all explode though when the funeral home showed up.

Laura called the twins and told them what was going on. She asked them though to keep it to themselves for right now. They were both worried about Laura. They knew how much Miss Peg meant to her. She assured them both though that she was all right. There was too much to do for her not to be. She had hoped she wouldn't have to do all of this for a long time though. Time to get going.

Someone had to go tell James. He wouldn't be able to go to the funeral but needed to be notified, nonetheless. Benjamin said he would go and tell him. He sure didn't think Laura should. That could get very ugly.

Chapter 62

James was not happy at all to see Benjamin. Prison obviously hadn't mellowed his temper any.

James: "What the hell do you want? I'm not signing any papers unless they're the ones to release me from this hellhole."

Benjamin: "I'm not here with any papers for you to sign. I'm here to tell you that your mother died this morning. She went peacefully in her sleep."

James looked down and got a nasty grin on his face.

James: "Peacefully, huh? That's too bad. I had hoped it would have been rough. So, what did she leave me in her will? Is it enough to buy my way out of here?"

Benjamin: "She left a trust to send money to your commissary account every month. That's all."

James: (Screaming) "WHAT!?? She was worth millions, and she didn't leave me anything? Who gets the factory and the house and all the property?"

Benjamin: "She sold the factory and all its assets about six months ago. Most of that money went to several of her charities. That's about all I can tell you. The rest is private information."

James: "She gave it all to that bitch Parker woman didn't she. Son of a bitch! I'll fight this. I have a right to my parents' properties. I'm a Martin! You can't do this to me!"

Benjamin: "First of all, Jim, you aren't *entitled* to anything. You won't be out of here any time soon, so none of it will do you any good anyway. Be thankful that she's left something to cover your snacks from the commissary. You put yourself in here; it's time you admit that. Your mother was very disappointed in you. She sure wasn't going to finance your bad behavior. I've said what I came here to tell you. I'll leave you to your stupid anger. You don't fool me...I'm the only one you think you can be nasty to. Fortunately I don't have to listen to it anymore. Goodbye, Jim. Enjoy your stay."

With that, Benjamin got up and left. James was still screaming when he left. He walked out with a big grin on his face.

Chapter 63

For the next week, the Martin household solemnly went through the motions like a well-oiled machine. Miss Peg had planned all of this not too long after Patrick died. She figured James would be in charge when she died, so she didn't want any surprises. She knew he would have no clue as to what to do. She didn't want something low-budget like James would have done. He would have pocketed the rest of any money left over from her funeral. As it stood, the wake would be quite the affair.

Margaret [Miss Peg] Martin, 63, passed peacefully in her sleep on June 1, 2011.

She was born September 18, 1947, in Kester to Roger and Stella Banks, both of whom preceded her in death.

She married Patrick Martin on January 13, 1980. He preceded her in death in 2004. She is survived by a son, James.

Miss Peg, as she insisted on being called, was a long loved member of the Kester community.

She was the co-owner of now Graham-Martin Metal Fabrication, where the employees earned above average wages.

She sat on the boards of several charities. She was her own silent charity, though. She served meals on Thanksgiving and gave generously to the Food Bank. She couldn't imagine any person going hungry if she could help it.

Many people were recipients of her generous heart. No one will ever know how many houses she kept from foreclosure, how many funerals she paid for, how many children got the education they deserved but couldn't afford.

Miss Peg had money, but instead of lake houses or fancy cars, she invested in the people of Kester.

She, along with her husband, Patrick, helped the scholarship funds in each of the high schools grow by leaps and bounds.

Her Garden and Holiday parties were memorable. To get an invitation to one or the other was an honor.

She will be greatly missed by anyone who ever crossed her path, either intentionally or by accident. Her quick wit and big smile that consoled many people will be what most people will miss the most.

Viewing will be Monday, June 6, 2011, from 3 p.m. to 7 p.m. at McCullough Memorial Chapel and at 10 a.m. Tuesday, June 7, 2011 before Graveside Services at 11 a.m. at Grace Serenity Gardens where she will be interred in the family mausoleum next to her husband.

The viewing went well beyond 7 p.m. Miss Peg had a lot of friends who wanted to say goodbye and pay their respects. The procession to the cemetery looked like a who's who in black SUVs, like a presidential motorcade. It stretched on for miles. Every domestic of all the people in the SUVs was there. They all worked for Miss Peg from time to time at one of her parties. The owners of just about every and any industry in Kester were there. She knew everyone. In her will, Miss Peg asked that Laura give the eulogy. Oh, another toughy.

Laura was still uncomfortable speaking. In court, she had only faced the Judge. The gallery was behind her. Here she'd have to face all these people. She could do it....for Miss Peg.

When it was time, she walked up to the podium. She had the eulogy written out, figuring it would be easier for her to get through it.

Laura: "Hello, everyone. I am Laura Parker. Instead of a minister, Miss Peg wanted me up here in front of you. You'll hear a tremble in my voice because I'm not a public speaker, and I was very close to Miss Peg and cared deeply for her."

"Miss Peg...everyone called or at least referred to her by that name. When I first met her, I called her Mrs. Martin like I had been taught, and she corrected me very quickly. She said, 'Mrs. Martin is my mother-in-law. I don't even want to be compared to her by using her name.' All I could say was, 'Yes, ma'am, Miss Peg.' (Laughter) I was eighteen. She hired me right after my father was killed. No one knew at the time that this would become a lifelong friendship, but it did. When my mother died, she was the first person I needed to tell. I'm not ashamed to say that my parents' funerals were some Miss Peg paid for. We tried to repay her, but she wouldn't have it. Her employees were her family. Actually, after seeing how some families treat one another she treated people she knew much better."

"When she took over Martin Metals a few of the men weren't happy that they had to work for a woman. She set them all straight immediately. She knew as much, if not more, of the inner workings of the company than those men did. She was...well...feared and respected after that."

"When she passed, we were in the process of planning parties for the 4th of July and Halloween. She loved to see people happy. It's true, she was the wealthiest woman in town but do you know where she spent Thanksgiving? At a unique soup kitchen she set up to feed anyone who wanted to have dinner with her. She just glowed dishing up those mashed potatoes. I'm happy to say a lot of people enjoyed that meal."

"Miss Peg...hmmm...her name now will only be used in passing and memories. Oh, those memories are so vivid. Vivid because you don't forget when someone loves you as much as she did. I saw her angry enough to raise her voice once in all the years I've known her. Even that anger was short-lived."

"I will miss my friend very much. There will never be another person like her."

With that, Laura sat down. There were a lot of tears that day. Many, many people would miss her.

Chapter 64

It was two weeks before Mr. Lancaster could come to the estate to read Miss Peg's will. It was true, Miss Peg was a multimillionaire. There was a lot to go through before the will could be read. That's a lot of money to move around and account for.

During this time, the staff continued their typical daily responsibilities. Joanne was only cooking for the staff right now, so Laura came up with an idea. She had Joanne make up individual meals to be sent to the homeless shelters. There were still a lot of people who were food insecure in Kester. Laura felt she was doing something Miss Peg would have done. The meals weren't fancy, but they were filling. These meals were delivered on Monday, Wednesday, and Saturday. This was something that could continue as long as the need was there. The whole kitchen staff was excited to do this. Charles and one staff member would deliver the meals.

On Thursday, June 16, Mr. Lancaster showed up to read Miss Peg's will. Everyone (except James) named got a call from his office to be there at 1 p.m. Everyone was seated around the table in the large dining room. The mood was somber. They all felt they needed to speak in a whisper. The only sound you really heard was the rubbing of cloth against the upholstered chairs.

Mr. Lancaster: "Hello, everyone. I am Sam Lancaster, Miss Peg's attorney. I've known the Martins for at least twenty-five years. Patrick had just taken over Martin Metals. I worked for a small firm. There were only three of us. They wanted someone that wasn't 'jaded yet' to handle their company and personal legal needs. The Martins, even then, were a wealthy and well-known family in Kester. All the head of the firm told me was, 'Don't mess this up. This could be worth a lot to us.' Well, I didn't mess up, I guess, because I'm still representing them....Oh, I'm now the head of the firm.

"When Patrick died, and Miss Peg took over at the factory, there ended up being a lot of legal wrangling. The Board—The Old Guard—didn't want to work for a woman. They didn't realize how much Miss Peg knew about the company or them. She knew all about them personally, too. She spoke to each Board member alone. She let each one know she knew about all the skeletons in each one's closet. If they still wanted to work there they would need to mind their Ps and Qs, or they would voluntarily or involuntarily leave. That quieted all of them—believe you me. She wasn't one to mess with.

"When she sold to Graham Industries recently, they tried, too, to take advantage of her because she was, this time, an elderly woman. You notice their name isn't the only name on the company. She made sure none of the employees were unduly affected. No one lost their seniority or pension. For the first three months after Graham took over, they had to pass everything through Miss Peg to get her approval. There are still stipulations in place that I don't think Graham will have problems implementing.

"Miss Peg was a force to be reckoned with. She was very knowledgeable but knew when to ask for someone's help. Under some circumstances, the help she gave—such as funerals-- would actually have been a hardship...monetarily. She and I worked things out to where she could continue to help people-- sometimes with large amounts-- and the recipient never had to worry that they may have had to declare that money as an income. She thought of everything.

"Now, you are all aware that the reason you are here is because she left you all something. About two months ago, Miss Peg and I went over all of this. Again she didn't want any one of you to be burdened with having to pay income taxes on anything she has left you. The amount I quote will be different than the actual amount you will receive. So as to not be a problem, the amount will include the income taxes. So, say you get $100. You'll receive a check for $100 and a check for $20. The extra $20 will be the amount you send to the IRS. I'll give you a filled-out form, so all you have to do is send that amount in with the form. It is your responsibility to do it as soon as possible to avoid any penalties. You're all smart people, so I know you'll follow the instructions. The amount over and above the amount I tell you will be what amounts to a gift. You don't pay taxes on a gift. If you have any questions after this, feel free to ask."

He looked around and cleared his throat.

"I will read off your names individually. When I have said your name, please come and get your envelope. I'll go through the staff first. After I've gone through all your names, if you wish, you may open your envelope. You'll see that it isn't necessary to do it right now, though…

Cynthia Brown
Mary Sanchez
Bethany Anderson
Joanne Peters
Nancy Perser"

"Now, you all meant the same to her. She cared for you all the same. So, in your envelope, you will find a check for $50,000. Again, the amount of the other check is what you will pay for the income tax."

All the women let out a loud GASP. They had no idea Miss Peg would leave them this much money. Everyone was crying at this point.

Mr. Lancaster: "Okay,

Benjamin Rose

Charles Testor"

"She left a comment for you two men as well."

"'Benjamin, you were more than a personal assistant. You were a friend and confidant. You knew things no one else knew and never would.'"

"'Charles, we spent time talking on drives when you took me sometimes—nowhere—in the middle of the night. I don't think there is a thing here you couldn't fix.'"

"'Thank you both. After Patrick died and this whole mess with James, you two kept me sane.'"

"In your envelopes, you'll find a check for $75,000."

Both men were dumbfounded. They were both single so this amount of money would go a long way.

Mr. Lancaster: "You seven people have worked for Miss Peg for many years. You know more about how this house is to run more than anyone. For a reason I will be explaining in a bit, the house needs to run and be maintained as you have done all these years. Miss Peg trusted you to do just that. None of you are losing your jobs for just that reason. You will be needed to perform your duties for many more years to come. I hope you all choose to stay."

"Now…

Elizabeth Parker Nance

Jeremiah Parker"

"There is another personal note from Miss Peg."

"'I had the honor and pleasure of watching the two of you grow up, pursue your amazing careers, and walk down the aisle to get married. I also bore the sadness of the tragedies you both had to endure at the hands of Patrick and James. Your strength and inner fortitude though has gotten you where you are today. I know your parents would be beaming with pride. I'm not your parent, but I am very proud of you. No amount of money will make up for what you have had to live through, but, you do deserve to have a good life. You *are* like my children.'"

"She wants to address any children you have first. There is a trust she has set up for any future children you may have. At each one's birth, $25,000 will be put in a college fund for them. You won't have to work two or three jobs to have the money to send them to school. By the time they're ready to go to college, this fund should be sufficient. If not, I, or one of my associates, will see that the money is there."

"Now, for each one of you. Now that you are both married and no longer living at home, you'll probably be looking for a house. Miss Peg wants to help with that. In your envelopes, you will find a check in the amount of $150,000. This should make a very nice down payment. I can reinvest this for you so it has a chance to grow even more if you like. It is up to you. She never could deal with what Patrick and James put you through but hopes this helps you move on to a comfortable life."

Elizabeth and Jeremiah just sat there, shocked. They had no idea they would receive anything. The amounts were more than they could ever have wished for.

Mr. Lancaster: "I don't even want to mention him, but legally I have to. James will get $150 per month put into his commissary account for as long as he is incarcerated. He has no legal standing to try and receive anything more. There...I got that bad taste out of my mouth."

"Now, Laura Parker. After all of this, I know you're wondering...*What about me?* Well, I doubt you thought about it like that though. Miss Peg loved you the most. The horrors you have lived through at the hands of her family were almost more than she could bear. You were a daughter and a dear, dear friend. I'm sure you realized how much you meant to her when she wouldn't let you completely quit working for her. She needed you around. She wanted to protect you, and when she couldn't, it almost killed her. Right after your attack, she came to see me to figure out how she could help you."

"She couldn't help you have any babies of your own, so she came up with an idea for maybe the next best thing."

At this point, Laura had a very quizzical look on her face.

Mr. Lancaster: "Laura, Miss Peg has left you the house and all the property. Hold on; there's much more to her idea. I will help you create a nonprofit to take care of foster children until they are able to be adopted. You will have social services staff that will live here along with the children twenty-four hours a day. All I need from you right now is the answer to whether or not you want a lot of little people running around here for you to take care of. You can give these children the love and attention they need until they are adopted. I have all the paperwork already drawn up. If you're interested, you only have to say 'yes' and give the home a name."

Laura was stunned. She could take neglected and unwanted children and give them all the love she held in her heart for what would have been her own children.

Laura: "YES! YES!"

Mr. Lancaster: "Wonderful. Now, Laura, can you think of a name for the nonprofit?"

Laura: "Oh, yes. 'The Miss Peg Foster Care Home.' Will that be okay?"

Mr. Lancaster: "I think that is perfect. Now, Miss Peg didn't want to just put you to work. You have an envelope, too. Inside is a check for $100,000. That is just for you, not to use for the foster home. There is a nice budget to maintain the home and grounds. You will receive a paycheck, too. As I told everyone at the beginning. No one is losing their jobs. You'll only leave if you choose. The house still needs to be maintained in its current condition. So, Ladies and Gentlemen, you can just continue where you left off. There will be some additions like children's beds and toys. Rooms need to be painted. You won't be doing that but will continue your previous duties. Miss Joanne, your duties will take on a new meaning. You'll be cooking for children and making birthday cakes and other treats for them. Are you okay with that?"

Joanne: "Oh, my, yes. It will be wonderful to have children's laughter in this house for a change."

Mr. Lancaster: "Benjamin, if you choose to stay, which I'm sure Laura hopes you do, you'll continue your duties for the home as you did for Miss Peg. There will be all amounts of money coming and going and different expenditures. Are you up for it?"

Benjamin: "I am. This will be happy work, and I love it. I wouldn't want to be anywhere else."

Mr. Lancaster: "Okay, is everyone on board? No one will fault you if you want to leave. This is an emotional time for everyone, and there will be some changes."

Mr. Lancaster: "Perfect. Now, Charles, you're an old bachelor like me. Think you can handle a bunch of children on a bus going and coming from school? You'll do much more than that, but that will be one of your duties. Are you ready?"

Charles: "Miss Peg mentioned just this scenario on one of our late-night car rides. I think she would have done just this had she lived. I was on board with her...I'm on board with Miss Laura as well."

Bethany: "I think I speak for everyone. We want to stay. Miss Peg would count on all of us to back Laura up in whatever she does here."

Mr. Lancaster: "Perfect. We can get started right away then transforming the house. Even though no one actually worked today, you will all get paid. You're all free to leave while I start tweaking some things here."

"I want to personally thank all of you for how you took care of Miss Peg through the years. At any given time, she fussed about each and every one of you. Your welfare meant a lot to her. She had been a dear friend to me for many years. She had confidence in me when some people doubted my abilities. The care you all took meant a lot to me...especially after Patrick died. You all made her smile. I want to thank you for that."

There were tears all around as they all left.

Mr. Lancaster: "It's still early, Laura. I have a man from Social Services I want you to meet. He will help you get this off the ground and tell you what the requirements are. I could call him and be here when he comes to talk to you."

Laura: "That would be perfect. I'm going to go say goodbye to everyone while you make the call."

Chapter 65

There were a lot of hugs all around as everyone left. For a sad occasion, everyone was actually giddy. Miss Peg took care of the people she most cared about, even after her death. Everyone was heading to the bank with their envelopes. Charles was tasked with finding a small van for transporting the children. For short trips, he would still use the car but had to find car seats that would go in and out quickly. That old codger was humming and had a big grin on his face. This would be the closest he'd ever be to being a grandpa, and he loved it.

Benjamin stayed back to go over plans with Mr. Lancaster and Laura. His ledger would look a whole lot different. He was pleased that Miss Peg gave him the reason to be able to stay.

Mr. Lancaster called Social Services. Jack Trainer, head of Social Services should be there any minute.

Laura walked back into the house and just stood there in the foyer and looked around. Wow, this was all hers. Miss Peg was always generous, but she never expected anything like this. AND BABIES! Well, children of all ages, actually. She could hardly wait to hold the first one in her arms. She was so excited she did a double fist bump in the air. Benjamin had come out of his office about that time and just stood there and smiled. This was going to be incredible.

They walked into Benjamin's office while Mr. Lancaster gathered all his paperwork from the dining room. The doorbell rang.

Mr. Lancaster: "I'll get it."

Laura and Benjamin were leaning over his desk, talking and laughing, when Mr. Lancaster and Jack Trainer walked into the room. They looked up from the papers on the desk, and Laura just froze. Jack Trainer had to be the nicest-looking man she had ever met. He was tall with dark, thick, wavy hair. His brown eyes lit up when he met Laura.

She couldn't speak. Mr. Lancaster looked at her, then looked at Jack and just smiled. Benjamin did the same thing. This would be interesting.

Mr. Lancaster: "Laura Parker, Benjamin Rose, this is Jack Trainer, the head of Social Services in town. He'll be instrumental in helping set up the home, bringing in children, and helping them get adopted. Jack, this is Laura. She's the owner of the home, and Benjamin is her personal assistant."

No one moved. Finally, Benjamin stepped up and shook Jack's hand, and signaled for Laura to do the same. That handshake though lasted a little longer.

Mr. Lancaster: "I'll tell you what. (That kinda broke the spell. Jack and Laura let go of each other's hand.) It's getting on in the day. Why don't we all go to dinner and get the discussion started? It'll be a more relaxed atmosphere, and to be honest, I'm really starving."

Everyone agreed. They'd meet at a local restaurant, have dinner and discuss "The Miss Peg Care Home" supposedly.

When everyone was sitting and drinks were ordered, the conversation stalled but only for a minute. Benjamin and Mr. Lancaster made sure Laura and Jack were seated across the table from each other so they would have to look at each other to talk. Some would say Benjamin and Mr. Lancaster had more up their sleeves than just the Home. There was a lot of smiling between those two. It looked like they hit a nerve.

Laura: "Jack, how long have you been the head of Social Services?"

Jack: "About ten years. I started out fifteen years ago as a social worker. I have taken care of a lot of children in that time."

Laura: "How much area do you cover?"

Jack: "All of Miami County."

Laura: "That's a lot of territory. Your kind of work then is pretty much a twenty-four-hour day, isn't it?"

Jack: "Yes, I've lost count of how many 3 a.m. calls I've made to remove a child from a bad situation."

Laura: "Must be frustrating for your wife to hear the phone at that hour."

AND THERE IT WAS!!

Jack: "Oh, I'm not married. No kids of my own, either. I devote all my time to helping someone else's children get a better, safer life. I don't see a ring on your finger, either."

Laura: "I've never had the time. I raised my brother and sister after our parents died. They were my first priority. I worked for Miss Peg and cleaned houses so I could be at home evenings with them. There was no time to date."

Jack: "So, you worked closely with her. That surely explains the home's name."

With tears in her eyes, Laura just shook her head.

Benjamin: "So, Jack, how do we start to be able to get these kids to our foster home?"

Laura looked at him and just glared. Mr. Lancaster just chuckled. There was definitely something more going on here besides social work.

Three weeks after the will was read the 4th of July was celebrated. Laura planned a party. It wouldn't be the whole town as Miss Peg wanted though. This one would be just family. Family was all the people, and their families who had worked for Miss Peg and now employees of the Foster Care Home. It was a month after Miss Peg died but they all had a reason to celebrate Some more than others.

Elizabeth though was saddened. At about the time Miss Peg died she thought she was pregnant but didn't say anything. She knew Miss Peg would have been overjoyed had she known. All the Parker children considered her their adoptive mother. She would have been a "grandma."

Chapter 66

Within a month of conceiving the idea of a foster home, things were coming together. Bedrooms (there were eight) were transformed with four-poster beds being replaced with cribs and twin beds. One of the rooms was left for the live-ins. There would be two there at all times. A total of six people so far had been vetted and would rotate. The children would get to know them all so they would feel safe and comfortable.

Toys were bought, and playground equipment was erected outside. Laura asked Bethany and Cindy to go shopping for the toys. They both had children, so they knew what to buy to get started. Not knowing the ages of the children coming made the purchases a little tricky. They just got things to hold them for a day or two....stuffed animals, cars, dolls...things of that nature. They did the same with clothes. They bought two outfits of each size to make sure they started out with something clean if they didn't have anything. One of the cribs was put in the room with the live-ins. They could care better for an infant that way.

Jack spent a lot of time there with Laura and Benjamin. He made sure all the safety features were in place for any age child that would come to the house.

Laura wouldn't be there twenty-four hours a day. That's why there were live-ins. She would be there every day though to make sure everything was being done. The original staff stayed on as she had hoped. There was a lot of activity.

Joanne still cooked the meals to be delivered to the shelters. Between her and Nancy, that kitchen ran like a clock.

All the staff were waiting for the first children to arrive. The thought was both sad and exciting. Exciting because they would have children in the house and sad for the same reason. The children would have been removed from an unhappy situation of some kind. They would be frightened and sad. It would take everyone to make them feel safe and loved. They had to make sure not to frighten the children more by everyone converging on them all at once. It would be a fine line between caring and scaring.

Jack spent a lot of time there instructing everyone on procedures. He'd be there with each child to start. The regular staff wouldn't be interacting that much with the children but they still needed the basics.

The paperwork to legally open this size facility was pretty overwhelming itself. Laura and Benjamin reviewed form after form with Jack to make sure everything was filled out correctly. Jack managed to sneak in a few dinners alone with Laura to supposedly go over more paperwork. Paperwork that could be done at any time. He had an ulterior motive though, obviously.

Chapter 67

The Miss Peg Foster Care Home officially opened on September 10. It was a Saturday so that all staff and community members would have a chance to tour the facility. Board members were chosen from the larger businesses to oversee everything. They would meet once a month to go over the legal part of the nonprofit. Their salaries were minimal. They usually didn't have anything to do anyway. Benjamin and Laura ran it all.

There was a large BBQ grill set up out back, and there were mountains of food. Laura just wanted people to see the home and understand what would go on. The turnout was terrific. The managers from a couple of retail stores agreed to donate things like diapers and formula. The toy store would donate toys so all children would have something to take with them when they left.

Laura was happier than she had been in a long time. And...Jack just told her the first children would be there tomorrow morning. He said "children" because there were three. They were three siblings to be taken from an unsafe home. The exact circumstances were insignificant. The important fact was that, thanks to this home, they would stay together instead of being sent to separate foster homes. A lot of foster parents don't want to take on multiple children all at once. They usually aren't equipped to do that. Miss Peg's Home was though. That was its main purpose. These three children were little, too. Two, four, and six. They would be put in one room to avoid any fears of being separated.

At the party Laura got some other good news; Elizabeth was pregnant with twins. Who'da thunk it? Everything was starting to be just really close to how Laura had hoped it would be. It was comical because Carl was strutting around like a proud rooster.

Also, at the party, Jack asked Laura if one of the female staff could go with him to get the children. Since they were so small, they might feel better with a woman. Laura decided not to go herself. She had no experience at this point with small children. Bethany said she would go. She had a lot of experience with small children. After all...she had seven.

Chapter 68

On Sunday morning, Charles took the van with Bethany to meet Jack to get the children. It took all Laura could do to keep the remaining staff from rushing the van.

Laura: "These babies are probably very scared right now. Let's not descend on them all at once. Watch from the windows so they can't see you. Everyone will get a chance to meet them They need to know they're safe first."

At about 10 a.m., the van pulled up. Laura went out to meet it. She was all smiles. She just wanted to scoop them all up in her arms but knew she, too, would have to restrain herself.

One at a time, they got unbuckled and taken out of the van. Laura's heart just exploded when she saw them. They had been taken out of their home just an hour ago. All three had been crying; their clothes were filthy, and so were they. Laura approached slowly.

Bethany: "Kids, this is the nice lady I told you would be taking care of you. She really wants you here."

Four-year-old Bobby ran up to her and wrapped his arms around her legs, and started crying again. Six-year-old Jerry wasn't sure what to do. Two-year-old Susie just held on around Bethany's neck. Laura was at a loss for words. These children had obviously been neglected. How could someone not care for them? She picked up Bobby and turned toward the house. Jack picked up Jerry. They all followed Laura into the house. She tried to put Bobby down, but he wasn't having it. Truth be told, this was the moment Laura had been waiting for. She just held on to him as long as he wanted. Jerry was the first to speak.

Jerry: "Are we gonna live here now?"

Jack: "Yeah, buddy. These great ladies will take care of you. You're safe here."

Jerry: "Okay. Can I ask something?"

Jack: "You sure can. What do you want to ask?"

Jerry: "Is this where we can get something to eat?"

Jack: "Sure is, little guy. Are you hungry?"

Jerry: "Well, Susie is. We didn't eat anything today or yesterday."

Laura's heart about fell out of her chest. These babies hadn't eaten in at least twenty-four hours. It had probably been longer. She got down to Jerry's eye level, still holding Bobby.

Laura: "Sweetheart, you will never have to worry about that ever again. There will always be plenty of food for you to eat. Do you like oatmeal?"

All three children chimed in…"YEAH!"

Laura: "Well, you all come with me. I'll show you the nice lady that cooks here. She's going to fix you all some oatmeal. You can have milk and juice, too, if you want."

Jack: "You may need to go light. I don't know how well they'll handle a lot of food."

Laura: "That is why I figured oatmeal. A small bowl will probably fill them up. Come on, kids, let's go get some oatmeal."

The three of them chanted "OATMEAL, OATMEAL, OATMEAL" as they bounced to the kitchen.

Unfortunately, they wouldn't be the only children that arrived dirty and hungry. Laura's heart would break every time. She was just happy she could fix some of that problem for some of the children.

Chapter 69

Over the following months the house filled up and got emptier. At Christmas, the first three children were on track to be adopted. A young couple that wasn't able to have children fell in love with those three munchkins. It took a couple weeks for them to settle in, but before anyone realized, all three were running around and laughing. Joanne's cooking helped. She was always sneaking them a cookie. Laura couldn't be happier with the outcome. She'd cry when each one left but knew this was the reason in the first place.

These months had seen Elizabeth's belly grow and grow. She wasn't happy with her size right now but, hey, twins. They couldn't tell their sexes by the ultrasound yet because they were all cuddled together. Didn't matter though. They appeared to be very healthy at this point.

At Christmas, Laura also got the shock of her life. Jack asked her to marry him. He was aware they wouldn't have any children of their own, but he didn't care. The children at the home fulfilled his needs. He let Laura know that. He had fallen in love with her big heart…. And oh, she said yes!

The home was never at full capacity. That was a good thing though. Some children had come to just stay a short time until either their parents were again able to have custody or a relative came forward to take the child or children. They never got three at a time though like the first time. It was usually one at a time.

In January, they got their first newborn. He was only there until the paperwork for his adoptive parents was finalized. His mother never wanted him, so, she gave him up at birth. Laura really had trouble handing him over to his new parents. That was the first time she had ever held a newborn. The sadness flooded over her again, like when she first found out she couldn't have children of her own. Her heart soon filled with joy, knowing this little guy was going to someone who really wanted him.

Chapter 70

Much to everyone's happiness, on February 18, Laura and Jack were married. This was a day Laura thought would never come. She was trembling when Jeremiah walked her down the aisle. Elizabeth...big as a barn...sat with Carl and Georgette in the first pew. Sitting next to her was again the picture of their parents. In spirit, David and Sharon were at all three of their children's weddings. The sadness, setbacks, and horrors the three children had endured over the last twelve years had hopefully come to an end. All were now educated with amazing careers, married to wonderful people, and now adding to their families.

On February 22, 2012, twins...Michael David and Elisa Sharon were born to Elizabeth and Carl Nance. The babies and mom are doing great.